Sexuality
A Developmental Approach
to Problems

Clinical Child Psychology Library

Series Editors: Michael C. Roberts and Annette M. La Greca

PARENT–CHILD INTERACTION THERAPY
Toni L. Hembree-Kigin and Cheryl Bodiford McNeil

SEXUALITY
A Developmental Approach to Problems
Betty N. Gordon and Carolyn S. Schroeder

Sexuality
A Developmental Approach to Problems

Betty N. Gordon

University of North Carolina at Chapel Hill
Chapel Hill, North Carolina

Carolyn S. Schroeder

Chapel Hill Pediatrics and
University of North Carolina at Chapel Hill
Chapel Hill, North Carolina

Plenum Press • New York and London

Library of Congress Cataloging-in-Publication Data

On file

ISBN 0-306-45039-9 (Hardbound)
ISBN 0-306-45040-2 (Paperback)

© 1995 Plenum Press, New York
A Division of Plenum Publishing Corporation
233 Spring Street, New York, N. Y. 10013

10 9 8 7 6 5 4 3 2 1

For our children, Sarah and Andrew Gordon and Mark and Matthew Schroeder. We wish them as much fun parenting as we have had.

Foreword

There are few things that stir up our culture more than sex, particularly sex and children. Sexual behavior in children represents, to far too many people, further proof of the moral decay of our society. Any issue that provokes as strong an emotional reaction as childhood sexuality is obviously in need of a rational discussion. The best features of thought and reason include their moderating influence on overheated and reaction emotions. Consequently, this book by Betty Gordon and Carolyn Schroeder represents a very important, and even brave, counter to irrationality.

When the Surgeon General of the United States is forced to resign because the words "children" and "masturbation" appear in the same sentence, you know that there is a great deal of misunderstanding about sexuality. My own evolution as a researcher in the area of child sexual abuse is a model of how naiveté can be corrected by knowledge.

Some of my early research in sexual abuse of children led me to realize that sexual behavior was a reliable marker of victimization in a relatively large percentage of children (Friedrich, Urquiza, & Beilke, 1986). My blinders to sexuality were evident in that I had not even hypothesized that to be the case in this early, exploratory research. When I realized how important sexual behavior was, several colleagues and I set out to interview parents and foster parents of sexually abused children more specifically. These adults were routinely quite reactive to our queries. For example, a caregiver denied that a boy exhibited sexual behavior. I was told that the boy's masturbation was not self-stimulation, but a function of wearing underpants that were too tight. I saw this as further evidence that parents and caregivers were as unused to thinking about sexuality and children as we were. The information we gathered formed the basis of the Child Sexual Behavior Inventory (Friedrich, Grambsch, Broughton, Kuiper, & Beilke, 1991).

I was initially surprised when data indicated that every sexual behavior we examined had been observed by mothers of children carefully screened for the absence of sexual abuse (Friedrich, Grambsch, Damon, Hewitt, Koverola, Lang, Wolfe, & Broughton, 1992). My surprise gave way not only to a renewed appreciation of the complexity of human behavior but also to the diversity of children and child-rearing practices. In addition, I now realize that sexual behavior is natural in children and exists at some level regardless of the child's experiences.

In the past three or so years, as our culture became more aware of and reactive to sexual abuse, my pediatric colleagues and I began to get numerous phone calls about the normalcy of a child's sexual behavior. More than once I have had to explain that two 4-year-olds showing each other their genitals is not a marker for sexual abuse. Recently separated parents interpreted their child's behavior following visits to the estranged spouse as possible sexual abuse. Our culture's discomfort with sexuality has resulted in unnecessary agitation and concern in some quarters. I would like all individuals who work with children to be reminded that, as the authors of this book state, "all children who masturbate, even to excess, have not been sexually abused."

This book is very timely. Our culture needs the information provided herein. Knowledge about sexuality reduces hysteria. It also reduces precocious sexual activity in teenagers (Klein & Gordon, 1991), despite what is said by opponents of sex education.

We have much more to learn. As the authors mention, far too much information about children's sexuality is based on parents' reports. However, parents are hardly the ones who can accurately report behavior that is increasingly private after the preschool years.

As a practicing clinician who deals daily with sexual abuse in all its manifestations, I was struck as well by how accurate and reassuring the knowledge accumulated in this book is. The vagaries of memory and what interferes with disclosure are discussed. Parents as well as referral sources (therapists included) often wonder about the treatment needs of sexually abused children. In keeping with our "societal schizophrenia" about sexuality, parents may be told to never bring it up or they may be told their child will be damaged forever. Gordon and Schroeder provide some clinically valid guidelines about how to help sexually abused children and what avenues to pursue.

In addition, it is extremely useful to have the authors' comprehensive survey such as this one about sexuality and mental retardation. I also appreciated the review of gender identity disorder and precocious puberty. Misinformation abounds regarding these biopsychosocial phenomena.

I consider this book a brave work, a book that can help add thought and reason to a long-ignored emotional subject area. Previous books on sexuality in children have suffered from being either too permissive or lacking an empirical and developmental base. We are often asked for input about sexual abuse, teenage sexuality, parenting by gays and lesbians, as well as the normal, "stuff-of-life," i.e., day-to-day sexual interests of and behavior in children. Parents and clinicians need information presented in a valid, objective manner if they are to know how to deal with and advise parents and teachers.

W. N. FRIEDRICH

Mayo Clinic
Rochester, Minnesota

REFERENCES

Friedrich, W. N., Grambsch, P., Broughton, D., Kuiper, J., & Beilke, R. L. (1991). Normative sexual behavior in children. *Pediatrics, 88,* 456–464.

Friedrich, W. N., Grambsch, P., Damon, L., Hewitt, S. K., Koverola, C., Lang, R., Wolfe, V., & Broughton, D. (1992). The Child Sexual Behavior Inventory: Normative and clinical comparisons. *Psychological Assessment, 4,* 303–311.

Friedrich, W. N., Urquiza, A. J., & Beilke, R. L. (1986). Behavior problems in sexually abused young children. *Journal of Pediatric Psychology, 11,* 47–57.

Klein, M., & Gordon, S. (1991). Sex education. In C. E. Walker & M. M. Roberts (Eds.), *Handbook of clinical child psychology* (rev. ed. pp. 933–949). New York: Wiley.

Preface

Around the time this book went to press, President Clinton fired Surgeon General Joycelyn Elders for talking straight about the sex education needs of our young people. This action reflects the difficulty our society has in acknowledging that sexuality is an inevitable part of growing up and an essential aspect of relationships. The paradox is that we resist talking openly with children about sexuality, but at the same time we expose them to media images that, through sexual innuendo and explicit depiction of sexual acts, implicitly encourage them to engage in sex.

Unfortunately, the mixed message we give children about sex makes it difficult for them to acquire reasonable attitudes and values about sexuality and decreases the likelihood that they will make responsible sexual decisions. The result is that more adolescents are becoming parents at younger ages and the number of young people infected with HIV and other sexually transmitted diseases is on the rise. Society's repressive attitude about sexuality also has directly and indirectly hampered research on sexual development and has made it difficult for clinicians to understand and deal with the sexual problems of children and adolescents.

In the late 1970s, when Charles I. Sheaffer, a pediatrician at Chapel Hill Pediatrics, asked (no, *insisted*) that we begin working with children who had been sexually abused, we began meeting with a community group made up of professionals from the social services and the law enforcement agencies. Under Dr. Sheaffer's guidance, the group reviewed the professional literature about sexual abuse with the goal of developing a coordinated community effort to help these children and their families. At that time, most of the literature consisted of case studies describing assessment and treatment procedures that had little or no theoretical or empirical basis. As a result, our work was often guided by anecdotal reports and personal judgment. The lack of research on normal sexual development and sexual problems of children, coupled with the awesome responsibility we felt in dealing with cases of sexual abuse, set the stage for our own research and clinical work in the area of children's sexuality.

As we look back over the past 15 years, we are impressed with how our research and that of others has caused us to continually reframe our clinical approach to children and sexuality. We have broadened our perspective on what is considered ''normal'' sexual behavior for children. We are far more cautious in making determinations of sexual abuse, recognizing that false allegations of abuse can be as devastating to the individuals involved as actual sexual abuse is for children. We have learned that the aftermath of discovering sexual abuse can be as harmful as the abuse itself. Finally, we have come to accept that our beliefs about sexuality and children will be constantly challenged and changed as more research is done and as society's attitudes and values change.

We wrote this book for mental health professionals in the hope that it would inform them of recent research findings, make them aware of the areas in need of more empirical work, and encourage them to rethink their approaches to children's sexual problems. Recognizing that yet another book about sexual abuse was not needed, we decided to take a broader perspective on children's sexuality, emphasizing a developmental understanding of sexual issues and problems, and the need for assessment and treatment of problems that are sensitive to the child's development status. Most important, we emphasize a ''scientist–practitioner'' approach to children's sexuality that applies the empirical work to the practical problems faced by the clinician.

The book begins with an examination of the normal course of sexual development, including the physical aspects of sexual development and how children understand and express their sexuality at different ages. Issues related to sexuality education and sexual abuse prevention are also discussed. Chapter 2 covers sexual problems of children and adolescents and the related psychological issues, including discussions of anatomical sexual errors, gender identity disorder, delayed or precocious puberty, and oversexualized and sexually aggressive behavior. The next three chapters focus on sexual abuse of children with an emphasis on current research on assessment and treatment. The chapter on assessment reviews the research on children's memory and suggestibility and presents a framework for gathering and organizing assessment data that we hope will help clinicians avoid some of the pitfalls encountered in evaluating children's reports of sexual abuse. The final chapter covers the sexuality of children and adolescents with mental retardation. We included this topic because, despite the fact that these youngsters are at very high risk for sexual problems, particularly sexual abuse, most clinicians are uninformed about this topic and are therefore reluctant to work with these patients. We hope the information included will dispel some of the myths surrounding sexuality and mental retardation and provide a clearer understanding of the important issues.

The writing of this book was influenced by many people. We are particularly grateful for the early work of Michael Rutter on normal sexual development, the systematic research of David Finkelhor on sexual abuse of children, and the work of Bill Friedrich on children's sexual behavior and the treatment of sexual abuse. We also acknowledge Lucy Berliner's clinical expertise and clear thinking, Karen Saywitz's developmental approach to interviewing children, and Steve Ceci's ingenious research on children's suggestibility. We also thank the lawyers and judges who have sought our help with particularly difficult cases. Our consultation around these cases has been invaluable in helping us clarify what we do and do not know. We are grateful to our colleagues at the University of North Carolina at Chapel Hill and Chapel Hill Pediatrics who have given us critical feedback about our work and continue to support our efforts. Finally, we owe a debt of gratitude to all the parents and children who have enthusiastically participated in our research and also to those who have given us the opportunity to help them through difficult times.

BETTY N. GORDON
CAROLYN S. SCHROEDER

Contents

Normal Sexual Development

Even the most sophisticated parents and professionals have difficulty acknowledging (much less discussing) the sexuality of children. This is illustrated by
the following situation that occurred in the family of a physician, his wife,
who was a nurse, and their three children. The mother was expecting their
fourth child, but despite repeated requests from the children for information
about the birth process, the parents had avoided discussing the topic. Finally,
when the baby was obviously due to arrive at any minute, the children (in
the father's absence) said, "Mother, please tell us how this baby is going to
get out." At this point, the mother gave them a detailed explanation and the
children asked her to repeat it a second time, saying, "We've got to get this
just right so we can tell Daddy. He doesn't know a thing about this!"

The child clinician often confronts issues of childhood sexuality through
questions from parents, teachers, and others who are involved in the lives of
children, about the normality of a child's interest in sexual matters, sexual
exploration, or other sexual behaviors. These questions are often directed at
determining whether the specific behaviors of a child are typical and to be
expected, or are an indication that the child may have been sexually abused
or has a sexual problem. Clearly, if these questions and concerns are to be
placed in proper perspective, the clinician must have some understanding of
development of sexuality in normal, nonabused children. This chapter reviews
what is known about normal psychosexual development, including sexual
behavior and knowledge of sexuality. This is followed by a discussion of
sexuality education and sexual abuse prevention for children. A summary of
normal sexual development (including both sexual knowledge and sexual
behavior) is shown in Table 1.1.

SEXUAL BEHAVIOR

The study of sexual development is clouded by cultural attitudes and values
about sexuality in general and about children and sexuality specifically. Much

Table 1.1   Normal Sexual Development

Sexual knowledge	Sexual behavior

Birth to 2 years

Origins of gender identity	Genital exploration
Origins of self-esteem	Penile erections and vaginal lubrication
Learns labels for body parts including genitals	Experiences genital pleasure
Uses slang labels	Touches other's sex parts
	Enjoys nudity, takes clothes off in public

3 to 5 years

Gender permanence is established	Masturbates for pleasure, may experience
Gender differences are understood	orgasm
Limited information about pregnancy and	Sex play with peers and siblings: exhibits
childbirth	genitals, exploration of own and others
Knows labels for sexual body parts but uses	genitals, attempted intercourse
slang	Enjoys nudity, takes clothes off in public
Uses elimination functions for sexual parts	Uses elimination words with peers

6 to 12 years

Genital basis of gender	Sex games with peers and siblings: role plays
Correct labels for sex parts but uses slang	and sex fantasy, kissing, mutual
Sexual aspects of pregnancy	masturbation, simulated intercourse, plays
Increasing knowledge of sexual behavior:	"doctor"
masturbation, intercourse	Masturbation in private
Knowledge of physical aspects of puberty by	Shows modesty, embarrassment: Hides sex
age 10	games and masturbation from adults
	Body changes begin: Girls may begin
	menstruation, boys may experience wet
	dreams
	May fantasize or dream about sex
	Interested in media sex
	Uses sexual language with peers

13+ years

Sexual intercourse	Pubertal changes continue: Most girls
Contraception	menstruate by age 16, Most boys are capable
Sexually transmitted diseases	of ejaculation by age 15
	Dating begins
	Sexual contacts are common: mutual
	masturbation, kissing, petting
	Sexual fantasy and dreams
	Sexual intercourse may occur in up to $3/4$ by
	age 18

of the work in this area has come from the Scandinavian countries where attitudes toward sexuality are quite permissive. Thus, the conclusions resulting from this work may not apply to children in the United States, where there are significant societal and ethical restrictions on our ability to gather empirical data on children's sexual behavior and development. Moreover, methodological issues have led to inconsistencies across the results of various studies. Studies that rely on parental report of children's sexual behavior, for example, report lower estimates of the frequency and nature of children's sexual experiences, than studies that include self reports. This inconsistency simply reflects the fact that much of children's sexual behavior is undiscovered by adults. Furthermore, the participants involved in the studies typically are white and from higher socioeconomic backgrounds. Thus, the results reported may not represent the full range or frequency of sexual behaviors exhibited by children from different ethnic or social class families. With these problems in mind, the next section reviews what little is known about children's sexual behavior.

Physical Aspects of Sexuality

Despite the difficulty of conducting research on sexual development, it is now commonly accepted among professionals that the physiology for sexual arousal and orgasm, and the capacity for a variety of sexual behaviors, appear to be present in children from birth or even before birth. We know, for example, that fetuses suck their fingers and toes, and that newborn male babies have penile erections, while female babies are capable of vaginal lubrication (Martinson, 1981). Moreover, sexual arousal in infants and young children, as well as in adults, is often associated with the rapid eye movement (REM) stage of sleep and thus is probably a universal phenomenon that occurs across the life span (Karacan, Rosenbloom, & Williams, 1970).

It is important to keep in mind, however, that infants and young children lack the cognitive capacity and experience that adults bring to sexual encounters; therefore this early autoerotic behavior is more appropriately thought of as "pleasure seeking" than sexual, and often appears to be primarily a reflex or a conditioned reflex if it occurs repeatedly and appears nonaccidental (Martinson, 1981).

Beginning with these early sexual behaviors, sexual development progresses throughout infancy and childhood, but with the exception of puberty, no developmental milestones have been clearly identified. The lack of clearly delineated stages most likely reflects the fact that there are few physical changes associated with sexual development in the years prior to the onset of puberty. For both boys and girls, for example, hormone production is small and there is little growth in gonads until adolescence (Tanner, 1962). In contrast to the lack of physical changes in childhood, the changes that occur during adolescence are tremendous. These changes happen over a relatively lengthy period of time (4 to 5 years for boys and 3 to 4 years for girls). Moreover, there is great variation in the age at which puberty begins, although the onset of puberty for girls is typically 18 to 24 months before the onset for boys (Rutter, 1970). In boys, for example, the average age of first ejaculation is about 14 years, with a range of from 10 to 16 years (Kinsey, Pomeroy, & Martin, 1948). In contrast, for girls, the average age of menarche is about 13 years, with a range of from 10 to 16½ years, however, breast development may begin much earlier (between 8 and 13 years) (Kinsey et al., 1948). There are many psychosocial factors associated with the age at which puberty occurs and these will be discussed in the section on sexual problems.

Masturbation and Other Sexual Behaviors

Despite the lack of physical changes prior to adolescence, much important development in the psychosexual arena occurs during early childhood. Children, especially during the preschool years (i.e., 2 to 6 years), are reported by parents to engage in a wide variety of overt sexual behaviors (Friedrich, Grambsch, Broughton, Kuiper, & Beilke, 1991). In a survey of parents of nonabused children aged 2 to 12 years, Friedrich et al. (1991) found that although some behaviors were reported relatively rarely (e.g., puts mouth on sex parts, inserts objects in vagina/anus, imitates intercourse, masturbates with object), all of the 44 sexual behaviors listed on their questionnaire were shown by at least some children.

Masturbation is probably the most common sexual behavior seen in young children (Routh & Schroeder, 1981). It has been observed in infants as young as 7 months (Martinson, 1981) and evidence suggests that even children as young as 2 or 3 (males especially) are capable of experiencing orgasm as a result of masturbation (Gundersen, Melas, & Skar, 1981; Kinsey et al., 1948). During the first two years of life, masturbation appears largely related to general curiosity about one's body. Gradually, however, children discover that genital stimulation results in particularly pleasurable sensations and masturbation begins to take on a decidedly erotic aspect.

There is some inconsistency among researchers about developmental trends in the incidence of masturbation. It is reported by some to increase among boys and girls in the years preceding puberty (although the rates are thought to be somewhat lower among girls) (Rutter, 1970), while others (e.g.,

Friedrich et al., 1991) report a decline in sexual behavior in general, and masturbation in particular, with age. It is likely that these conflicting results reflect the fact that older children are more aware of societal views about the acceptability of sexual behavior, and exercise restraint in where and when they engage in these behaviors. Thus, studies that rely on parental report (such as Friedrich et al., 1991) are more likely to find decreases in masturbation and other sexual behaviors with age than those that include self-report.

Despite the fact that masturbation is such a common sexual behavior in children, many parents still react negatively to it and may even punish their children if they are caught touching themselves (Calderone & Johnson, 1983). Parents who accept masturbation in their preschool children may become uncomfortable with this behavior as it assumes a more adult sexual quality (Klein & S. Gordon, 1991). Yet there is no evidence that masturbation is harmful, and in fact it may be considered an appropriate and adaptive sexual outlet for many people.

Sexual Play

The point at which children first become aware of sexual behavior as an interpersonal phenomenon is unclear. Obviously, cultural attitudes and values greatly influence our understanding of this issue. It is likely that estimates of the age of onset of children's sexual encounters with others will be much earlier in societies that hold more permissive attitudes than in those with more restrictive perspectives. Nonetheless, we know that in the context of caregiving and nurturing, sensual and possibly erotic encounters between the infant and mother (and other caregivers) begin at birth and continue throughout the early years. Indeed, these experiences of touching and physical affection are critical for the healthy development of the child.

It is also common knowledge that preschool children are very curious about their own and others' bodies, and that given the opportunity, they will engage in sexual exploration with other children. Gundersen et al. (1981), for example, reported a study of the sexual behavior of Norwegian children (ages 3–7) in a preschool setting where only coercive sexual interactions and inserting objects into body openings were forbidden. The teachers reported that sexual play was very common among the children and involved body exploration, genital manipulation, and attempts at sexual intercourse.

Despite the more restrictive attitudes toward sexuality in the United States, sexual play among children appears to be a very common phenomenon in this country as well. Lamb and Coakley (1993) recently reported that 85% of their sample of college women recalled engaging in sexual games during childhood, at an average age of 7.5 years. Only 56% of these experiences were ever discovered by parents or other adults.

Lamb and Coakley (1993) provide information about the nature of these childhood sexual encounters. Most of the contacts were with friends (86%) and were about equally divided between same and opposite sex experiences (56% vs. 44%, respectively). Over 40% of the activities reported involved fantasy sexual play or other activities in which children experimented with sexual stimulation, including sexual intercourse, rape, prostitution, and strip shows. Playing "doctor" and exposing one's genitals were also reported to be common activities. Over one third of the games involved genital fondling, and a few included oral–genital contact, insertion of objects in genitals, or attempts at sexual intercourse. This study suggests that sexual games are very common among children and may involve relatively adultlike sexual activities. Moreover, Lamb and Coakley (1993) conclude that although it is commonly believed that childhood sexual games are thought to be largely motivated by curiosity, many children find them a source of sexual stimulation and excitement.

The sexual experiences reported by Lamb and Coakley (1993) were largely considered "normal" and positive by the participants, but some of these experiences (up to 43%) were reported to involve coercion (persuasion, manipulation, or force) of some type. These coercive encounters were more likely to involve cross-gender games, and not surprisingly, the more coercion reported, the less likelihood there was that the experience was perceived as being normal. Lamb and Coakley (1993) conclude that sexual interactions that are coercive, and might even be considered abusive, occur within the context of "normal" childhood sexual games, especially when girls and boys play together. Moreover, these coercive encounters are not very likely to be reported or otherwise discovered by adults.

Sexual encounters between siblings appear to be similar to those with friends in the types of activities involved, the motivations associated with the interactions, the ages at which they occur, and the perception of the experiences as relatively positive or normal. In a study of 796 college students, Finkelhor (1981) reported that sexual incidents were equally likely to occur at all ages (0 to 13+ years), although there were age differences in the types of activities in which the children engaged. Younger children were more likely to exhibit their genitals than older children, and older children were more likely to engage in attempted or actual intercourse than younger children. The respondents reported engaging in mutual masturbation equally across the ages.

Sex between siblings appears to occur much less frequently than sex between friends. Estimates of the prevalence of sibling sexual encounters range from 9% (Lamb & Coakley, 1993) to 13% (Finkelhor, 1981). It is likely that the lower rate of sex between siblings reflects two factors: (1) the age differential that typically exists between siblings may inhibit the occurrence of sexual interactions; and (2) retrospective reporting of sex between siblings may be influenced by knowledge of the incest taboo. In his survey of college students, Finkelhor (1981) found that the majority of sibling sexual encounters (67%) reported were initiated by older brothers. Moreover, the average age difference between participants for all the sexual encounters reported in this study of siblings was 2.9 years.

Despite the age differential of siblings, their sexual play does not appear to be any more likely to be coercive than sexual play between friends. In Finkelhor's (1981) sample, which included both males and females, one-quarter of the encounters reported were accompanied by force of some kind, and girls were predominantly the victims in these cases (82% vs. 18% for males). Again, it is not surprising that these coercive experiences were more likely to be perceived as being negative than more mutual encounters.

Finkelhor (1981) examined the question of the extent to which sexual play in childhood affects later adjustment. He found that the women in his study who reported having had sibling sexual experiences, regardless of the nature of the experience (e.g., positive or negative) were more likely to be sexually active than those who had not had this type of sexual encounter. Positive sexual experiences with siblings, particularly those that occurred later (i.e., after age 9) had apparently healthy effects on sexual self-esteem. These women were more comfortable with their bodies and with their sexual activity as adults. In contrast, sexual experiences that involved a significant age differential between the siblings, especially those that occurred before age 9, were associated with lower sexual self-esteem. Recall that it is likely that these experiences involved some degree of coercion or force.

Taken together, the work on sibling and peer sexual encounters suggests that "normal" sexual contact among children occurs on a continuum, and that the differentiation between sexual play and sexual abuse is not always clear. Children's sexual games can range from reciprocal encounters that are motivated by curiosity, are positively perceived, and are associated with better self-esteem and later sexual functioning, to coercive encounters, often involving the use of force, that resemble sexual abuse, and are associated with poorer adjustment.

Sexual Exploration with Adults

Although the data on sexual play among children may not be surprising, it has also been demonstrated that nonabusive sexual encounters between children and adults are quite common. In a survey of 576 families with children aged 2 to 10 years in the United States by Rosenfeld, Bailey, Siegel, and Bailey (1986), parents reported that nearly 90% of 2- to 4-year-olds had recently touched their mothers' genitals and/or breasts, and that approximately 60% had touched their father's genitals. They also found that although this behavior decreased with increasing child age, close to one-half of the 8- to 10-year-olds had recently touched their mothers' breasts or genitals, while 20 to 25% had touched their fathers' genitals. The authors conclude: "Clearly, if all children who touched their parent's genitals were removed from their homes, we would have a lot fewer children living with their parents" (Rosenfeld et al., 1986, p. 483)!

Two studies, involving self-selected, nonclinical, and noncriminal samples, have reported that erotic feelings and a variety of sexual activities (including sexual intercourse, mutual masturbation, and oral sex) occur among family members more commonly than is generally thought (Nelson, 1981; Symonds, Mendoza, & Harrell, 1981). The sexual encounters reported by these subjects did not necessarily have a negative or damaging effect on the children or other family members involved. Several factors appeared to be associated with the perception of these experiences as positive or negative. These included: (1) the age of the child when the experience occured; (2) the age differential between the participants; and (3) the extent to which the encounter was mutual or forced. Thus, issues of power and freedom of choice appear to be important in determining how these experiences were perceived (Nelson, 1981). For instance, when a young child is involved in a sexual encounter with an older child or adult, and the child is manipulated or coerced into engaging in the sexual activity, the experience is more likely to have a negative impact on that child. Conversely, when older children and adults engage in mutually acceptable sexual behaviors, the experience may be perceived more positively.

A framework provided by Gil (1993) is helpful in distinguishing normal sexual play from that which might indicate a more serious problem. This framework focuses assessment on: (1) age and physical size differences between participants, with greater differences being more problematic; (2) differences in relative status or position of authority; (3) whether the sexual activity is consistent with developmental norms; (4) dynamics of the sexual activity, including whether coercive tactics are used, and the motivations and feelings associated with the activity.

Adolescent Sexual Behavior

Although there is limited research on sexuality in young children, adolescent sexuality has received a great deal of attention. The issue that is probably of greatest concern to parents and professionals in the area of adolescent sexuality is the age at which teens begin to engage in sexual intercourse. The average age at which adolescents become sexually active has decreased rapidly in recent years; research indicates that many adolescents first engage in sexual intercourse at about 12 years of age (Finkel & Finkel, 1981; Scott-Jones & White, 1990). It is estimated that by the end of adolescence more than 80% of males and 70% of females are having sexual intercourse (Hayes, 1987).

The early onset of sexual intercourse is seen as problematic because of its relationship to children's psychosocial development. For example, early onset of sexual activity is associated with greater involvement in delinquent behavior (Elliott & Morse, 1989). Moreover, teens who engage in sexual intercourse earlier are less likely to use effective methods of birth control and thus, are at higher risk for unintended pregnancy than those who wait until they are older (Scott-Jones & White, 1990). Further, teenage parents are more likely to drop out of school, thus setting up a series of long-term economic disadvantages and other negative life consequences (White & DeBlassie, 1992). Because research has shown that these events appear to be causally related, Rutter and Rutter (1993) refer to early sexual activity among teenagers as a ''turning point'' that can significantly shift the course of one's life trajectory. Thus, it is clear that understanding the factors that predict early sexual activity among teens is important for planning both prevention and intervention programs.

A variety of factors have been shown to be associated with the onset of sexual activity among teenagers. Scott-Jones and White (1990) interviewed teenagers between $12^{1}/_{2}$ and $15^{1}/_{2}$ years of age regarding their sexual behavior. They found that the adolescents who were more likely to be sexually active were those who: (1) had less highly educated mothers; (2) had a boyfriend or girl friend; (3) had lower educational expectations (i.e., did not intend to go to college); and (4) were at the upper end of the age range of the sample. In addition to these factors, White and DeBlassie (1992) indicate that factors related to family functioning, such as authoritarian parenting, poor communication about sexuality, and having older siblings who are sexually active, also may be important in the prediction of early sexual activity.

One can conclude from this work that the timing of sexual behavior in adolescence is terribly important in determining the course of life in adulthood. Early sexual activity is associated with increased risk of pregnancy, which in turn results in a great variety of negative economic and social consequences that impact the larger society as well as the individual teenager. It is assumed that sex education programs could prevent much early sexual activity, and it is commonly accepted that teenagers desperately need sex education. Yet parents and professionals continue to argue about what sex education should consist of, and perhaps more important, who should be responsible for doing it. Information about what children of different ages know and do not know about sexuality can help to inform this debate.

KNOWLEDGE OF SEXUALITY

The fact that children are known to engage in sexual behavior alone and in interaction with others from an early age does not necessarily mean that they have knowledge or understanding of sexual facts. Again, research in this area is inevitably biased by the culture in which it is conducted. It is important to note that the research reviewed in this section was conducted primarily in the United States, and therefore reflects the prevailing attitudes (considered to be relatively restrictive) in this country.

Early studies of children's knowledge of sexuality focused on the development of gender identity (e.g., Slaby & Frey, 1975) and the extent of children's understanding of pregnancy and birth (e.g., Bernstein & Cowen, 1975). In general, these studies have found a developmental progression in children's understanding of gender and the birth process, with younger children having incomplete and inaccurate knowledge and older children having a more accurate understanding of these topics. For example, studies of the concept of gender suggest that children first understand that gender is permanent (i.e., a girl always was and always will be a girl) and only later understand that gender is determined by one's genitalia (McConaghy, 1979).

More recent work indicates that children's knowledge of sexuality generally increases with age, but age differences may vary depending on the area of sexuality assessed, the gender of the child, the sexual attitudes of the parents, and the socioeconomic status of the family (Bem, 1989; Gordon, Schroeder, & Abrams, 1990a). Gordon et al. (1990a), for example, assessed knowledge of a variety of sexual topics in 2- to 7-year-olds from a range of social classes. They found that lower-class children had less knowledge about body parts and functions, pregnancy and abuse prevention, than did children from middle and upper class families. Although Gordon et al. (1990a) did not find differences between boys and girls in sexual knowledge, others have reported gender differences. Bem (1989) reported that girls knew as much about genitalia at 3 years as they knew at 5 years, whereas knowledge of genitalia among boys increased gradually with age. Moreover, significantly more girls knew what "vagina" meant than did boys (58% vs. 15%), but boys and girls knew "penis" equally well. Other work has shown that even very young children can be quite knowledgeable about certain aspects of sexuality (e.g., body parts and functions, gender differences), while knowledge about other areas (e.g., sexual intercourse, pregnancy, and birth) may be lacking even in older children (Gordon et al., 1990a; Waterman, 1986).

The relationship between children's sexual knowledge and their sexual behavior is not clear. Several studies suggest that sexual experience does not always lead to increased sexual knowledge-understanding. In their study of Norwegian preschool children, Gundersen et al. (1981) found that although the children were observed to engage in relatively sophisticated sexual behavior (including attempts at sexual intercourse), their questions focused on pregnancy, childbirth, and anatomical differences between boys and girls; understanding of sexual terminology was not demonstrated until at least 4 years of age. Similarly, Gordon, Schroeder, and Abrams (1990b) examined differences in the sexual knowledge of children who had been sexually abused (and thus were assumed to be sexually experienced) and nonabused children who were matched for age and social class. No differences were found between the two groups in knowledge of any area of sexuality assessed, including adult sexual behavior.

Taken together, these studies suggest that, at least in the area of sexuality, more experience is not necessarily accompanied by greater understanding. It is also possible, however, that knowledge and experience are mediated by parental attitudes toward sexuality. In the Gordon et al. (1990a) study, for example, children with less knowledge had parents who reported more restrictive attitudes toward sexuality and had done less sex education with their children.

Studies of teenagers' knowledge and use of contraceptives also suggest that attitudes are important in the relationship between sexual knowledge and behavior. Scott-Jones and White (1990) found that although the majority of their sample of young adolescents knew which contraceptive methods were most effective (i.e., the pill and condoms vs. withdrawal), those who were sexually active tended not to use these more effective methods; 31% reported using withdrawal (a noneffective method). Other work suggests that those adolescents who are at highest risk for unwanted pregnancies (those who are sexually active at younger ages) are least likely to perceive a responsibility for use of effective contraception (Morrison, 1989; Reis & Herz, 1989).

In summary, this work indicates that sexual experience and behavior typically precede knowledge and understanding, at least among younger children. The fact that children engage in sexual behavior before they have a clear understanding of what it is all about places them at high risk for a variety of adverse experiences which can impact negatively on their development.

Additionally, although many adolescents have sexual knowledge, this does not always influence their behavior. The discrepancy between knowledge and behavior indicates that we have much to learn about how to effectively educate children about sexuality. The next section examines issues related to the topics of sex education and sexual abuse prevention.

SEXUALITY EDUCATION

Sexuality education in its broadest sense involves the teaching of attitudes, values, and feelings about being male and female, as well as learning about anatomical parts and functions of the body. Children also must be taught the skills to enable them to make good decisions in the sexual arena. Parents, because of their ongoing contact with children, are the primary sex educators for their children, especially in the early years, even if they do not actively provide information. Moreover, most teenagers view their parents as influential in determining their attitudes and values about sexuality and prefer sex education to come from parents (Sanders & Mullis, 1988). Thus, children's knowledge of sexuality is clearly going to be related to the information parents have provided. Most parents, however, do not discuss all aspects of sexuality with their children. Most commonly, parents talk with children about pregnancy and the birth process but do not discuss sexual intercourse, sexually transmitted diseases, birth control, or sexual abuse, the very topics about which children, and especially adolescents, need information. Because many parents do not provide their children with sexual information, children are likely to receive such information from peers and public media, such as television, magazines, movies, and advertising, which is likely to be inaccurate, confusing, and may even be damaging.

Parents may be uncomfortable talking about sex with their children for a number of reasons, including their own attitudes about sexuality and their own experiences with sex education as children. Many parents indicate that their children are too young to understand, do not need sexual information, or may be harmed by it. Klein and Gordon (1991) suggest that two prevailing myths about sex education influence parents' decision not to provide information about sexuality to their children: (1) Knowledge is harmful and will overstimulate children to participate in more sexual activity at an earlier age, and (2) Children already know all there is to know, so why teach them?

The empirical evidence contradicts both of these myths. Provision of sexual information is actually associated with postponement of sexual activity by teenagers and more responsible sexual behavior when they do become sexually active (Klein & Gordon, 1991). Moreover, research clearly indicates that prior to adolescence, children do not understand many important aspects of sexuality despite the fact that they may be engaging in a variety of sexual behaviors. It is our opinion that providing sexual information enables children to make more responsible decisions regarding their sexual behavior.

Although some parents and professionals may be concerned about giving children too much information, too early, this is difficult to do. If children are told more than they want to know or are given information that they do not understand, they will simply "tune out" (Klein & Gordon, 1991; Martinson, 1981). Conversely, children also will seek out (although not necessarily from parents) and assimilate information when they are interested in and ready to learn about a particular topic. In general, we believe it is better to err in the direction of giving more rather than less information, but it is important that parents view sex education as an ongoing process rather than a "one time effort" and gear the information to the child's developmental level.

Parents should not necessarily wait for their children to ask the appropriate questions. For a variety of reasons, many children do not initiate conversations about sex, so parents must respond to behavioral cues that their children are "ready" for sexual information. Answering children's questions and responding to their sexual behavior in a simple, nonjudgmental manner that is appropriate to the child's developmental level can serve to satisfy curiosity about sex and decrease the need for sexual experimentation (Gordon & Snyder, 1983). Parents often become upset when they discover their children engaging in sexual exploration (alone or with peers or siblings), and do not know how to handle the situation. The discovery of this exploration can be viewed as an opportunity to have a "teachable moment," that is, that the child is ready to learn. We have found it effective to say to the child, "I can see you are curious about your body. I have a book that we can look at together, and then we can talk about it." In this way, parents can satisfy their children's normal curiosity about sexuality while setting limits on their behavior.

Sex education for children is most appropriately viewed as an ongoing process that begins at birth and continues throughout the course of development. By understanding normal sexual development (see Table 1), parents and clinicians can more easily determine what information is needed by children at different ages. Suggestions for what to teach children at different ages are outlined in Table 1.2.

Table 1.2   Information for Parents to Teach Children from Birth to 13+ years

Birth to 2 years

Body Parts and Functions

Provide correct labels for body parts including male or female genitalia when child or parent is touching each part. Provide simple information about basic body functions. Allow child to explore all his or her body parts.

Gender Identity

Learning about gender begins at birth when baby boys are dressed in blue and girls in pink. Parents provide guidance about this topic by their choices of toys, clothing, activities, and the behaviors of the child they choose to notice. Gender stereotypes are pervasive in our culture but flexibility is healthy. It's OK for boys to play with dolls and girls to play with trucks. Begin to teach the child what is special about being either a girl or boy.

Sexual Abuse Prevention

Children must first learn about body parts and functions before they can learn protection of genitalia. The best prevention at this age is close supervision.

3 to 5 years

Body Parts and Functions

Continue to use proper labels for body parts including male and female genitalia. Teach child about functions of genitalia including both elimination and reproduction.

Gender Identity

Talk about the physical differences between boys and girls. Reinforce the idea that each child is special and has unique characteristics including being a girl or boy.

Sexual Abuse Prevention

Genitalia are private parts and no one should touch them for purposes other than health or hygiene. Child should not touch anyone else's private parts. Explain that these rules apply to friends and relatives as well as strangers. Say "no, my parents told me not to do that" and get away. Tell someone if this happens and keep telling until child finds someone who will help. Make a list of who to tell. Begin to teach assertiveness skills. Practice saying "no" and telling. Allow your child to say "no" in other situations that are uncomfortable for him or her (e.g., "Give Grandpa a big kiss"). Child should know not to go with a stranger under any circumstances. Explain why and make sure child knows what a stranger is. Practice "what if" role plays.

Sexual Behavior

If child is caught in sex play with another child, use it as a "teachable moment." Explain that insertion of objects into body openings may be harmful and is prohibited. Child should learn that masturbation is a "private" behavior. Teach about appropriate and inappropriate words.

Table 1.2   (Continued)

6 to 12 years

Body Parts and Functions

Child should have complete understanding of sexual, reproductive, and elimination functions of body parts. All children need information on the changes that will come with puberty for both sexes, including menstruation and nocturnal emissions.

Gender Identity

Gender identity is fixed by this age. Encourage both boys and girls to pursue their individual interests and talents regardless of gender stereotypes.

Sexual Abuse Prevention

Discuss the child's conceptualization of an abuser and correct misperceptions. Identify abusive situations, including sexual harassment. Practice assertiveness and problem-solving skills. Teach children to trust their body's internal cues and to act assertively in problematic situations. Explain how abusers, including friends, relatives, and strangers, may manipulate children.

Sexual Behavior

Talk about making decisions in the context of relationships. Provide information about birth control and sexually transmitted diseases (including AIDS).

13+ years

Body Parts and Functions

Discuss health and hygiene. Provide more information about contraceptives and sexually transmitted diseases, especially AIDS. Provide access to gynecological exam for girls.

Gender Identity

While boys and girls are able to do many of the same things, reinforce the idea that there are special aspects of being male or female. Talk about the differences between girls and boys in social perception. Males tend to perceive social situations more sexually than girls and may interpret neutral cues (e.g., clothing, friendliness, etc.) as sexual invitations.

Sexual Abuse Prevention

Teach teens to avoid dangerous situations (e.g., walking alone at night, avoiding certain parts of town). Discuss dating relationships and in particular date/acquaintance rape and its association with alcohol and drug use. Let your teenager know you are available for a ride home *anytime* he or she finds himself or herself in a difficult or potentially dangerous situation. Enroll your child in a self-defense class.

Sexual Behavior

Share your attitudes and values regarding premarital sex. Provide access to contraceptives, if necessary. Accept your teenager's need and desire for privacy. Set clear rules about dating and curfews.

Klein and S. Gordon (1991) provide guidelines about important topics for effective sex education for professionals who are working with parents (see also Koblinsky, 1983). These include:

1. *What is normal and abnormal?* Any sexual idea, fantasy, dream, or wish is considered normal. There is tremendous variation in what society considers normal sexual behavior. Mental health professionals can reasonably assume that compulsive, exploitive, guilt-ridden, or unpleasurable sexual behavior is abnormal. The use of coercion, manipulation, or force in sexual encounters is never appropriate.

2. *How to handle masturbation?* Masturbation causes no physical or mental harm unless it is accompanied by guilt, is compulsive, or is not pleasurable. All children and adults are likely to engage in masturbation at some time and it can be a very adaptive expression of sexuality. Masturbation is best handled by teaching children to do it in private.

3. *What about the size of sexual organs?* Penis size is irrelevant to sexual satisfaction, although many boys worry that their penis may be too small. Similarly, breast size varies tremendously and is not related to sexual satisfaction. Girls may wonder if their vagina is too small or too large to accommodate their partner's penis. However, the vagina is quite elastic and can stretch to accommodate the birth of a baby.

4. *Will I be (or am I) homosexual?* Many people feel attracted to the same sex at one time or another and many youngsters engage in same-sex activities during childhood and adolescence. This does not necessarily mean that they are homosexual. The causes of homosexuality are not clear, but parents can be assured that there is little they can do to cause or prevent homosexuality. Moreover, there is general agreement among clinicians that homosexuality is not in itself unhealthy.

5. *How do I present a balanced perspective on sex?* Children can be greatly influenced by the preponderance of sexual messages presented in the mass media and parents should be encouraged to put sexuality in perspective. Sex is not the most important thing in life. Discussion of the relationship between love and sex is important.

6. *What about nudity in the home?* Parental nudity is an aspect of sexuality that varies tremendously among families. There is nothing inherently wrong with bathing with children or otherwise appearing nude in front of them. These activities may elicit questions from children and provide opportunities for parents to provide important information. By age 5 or 6, children naturally develop a sense of modesty and parents who are sensitive to their child's cues will begin to limit these activities.

SEX ABUSE PREVENTION

With the increase in reports of sexual abuse of children, teaching children personal safety skills has become an increasingly important aspect of sexuality education. Yet, many parents do not discuss sexual abuse with their children, and when they do so it is likely to be in terms of "stranger danger" rather than personal safety rules or child sexual abuse. Parents give a variety of reasons for not talking with their children about sexual abuse. In a summary by Wurtele and Miller-Perrin (1992), the most common reasons were: (1) subject is too difficult to discuss; (2) topic might frighten child; (3) child is too young for discussion; and (4) need for discussion has not occurred to parent. It is also likely that parents' hesitancy to discuss sexuality in general inhibits discussions of child sexual abuse or limits these discussions to nonsexual aspects of personal safety.

Although parents may be willing to participate in teaching abuse prevention skills to their children, it is likely that they, as well as their children, need information about sexual abuse. Many parents, for example, do not know or do not know how to tell their children that most sexual abuse is perpetrated by someone known to the child (Wurtele, Currier, Gillispie, & Franklin, 1991). Providing parents with the information they need to educate their children can improve parents' ability to protect their children (e.g., providing better supervision, changing sleeping arrangements, checking on day care centers, etc.) as well as increase children's personal safety skills (Wurtele & Miller-Perrin, 1992). Wurtele and Miller-Perrin (1992) suggest that the information provided to parents be expanded to include how to recognize symptoms of sexual abuse and how to respond to a disclosure. Moreover, parents need to know that children who have good self-esteem, problem-solving skills, and sexual knowledge are better able to protect themselves from sexually exploitive situations.

Involving parents, in combination with teaching behavioral skills (e.g., use of role play, modeling, reinforcement to teach personal protection, recognition of exploitive situations, etc.) has been demonstrated to be an excellent way to approach sexual abuse prevention, especially for preschool children (e.g., Wurtele, Kast, & Melzer, in press; Wurtele et al., 1991). It is important to note, however, that parents of children who are most at risk for sexual abuse (e.g., those from dysfunctional families, or who are socially isolated) are least likely to participate in such programs. For these children, classroom based programs are essential.

The earliest classroom-based prevention programs were generally de-

signed for elementary school aged children. When these programs were trans-
fered to preschools, they did not take into account the cognitive–developmental
level of these younger children. The result was that preschool children often did
not understand key concepts and did not show long-term gains in knowledge or
the ability to use prevention skills appropriately (Kolko, 1988; Repucci &
Haugaard, 1989). Moreover, some of these programs may even have had
negative effects, such as increasing the frequency with which children negatively interpreted positive situations (e.g., bathing, cuddling, physical examinations) or insisted that they could say "No" to anything and anyone (Repucci &
Haugaard, 1989).

To be effective, educational programs must recognize differences in
how children at various developmental levels conceptualize sexual abuse.
Preschoolers, for example, have difficulty understanding that someone they
love could hurt them and are not able to discriminate good and bad physical
contact. It has also been demonstrated that younger elementary school-aged
children are often unsure about the nature of sexual abuse and tend to view
perpetrators as "bad people," strangers, or someone close to their own age,
whereas preadolescent children understand that sexual abuse involves sexual
touching, but view perpetrators as older "mentally ill" or "sexually deviant"
people (Wurtele & Miller, 1987).

Current work indicates that prevention programs can be successful, even
for preschool children, when they include behavioral techniques such as modeling, guided practice, and reinforcement of appropriate responses (Wurtele,
1990; Wurtele, Kast, Miller-Perrin, & Kondrick, 1989). Wurtele and Miller-
Perrin (1992) have summarized the important components of sexual abuse
prevention programs. Programs for very young children should focus on teaching the simple idea of protection of private parts, rather than "good touch,
bad touch, and confusing touch," as the latter concept is beyond the capabilities
of preschool children (Miller-Perrin & Wurtele, 1988). Teaching the importance of disclosure ("Tell someone") is also considered a critical component
of programs for young children, because it is unlikely that all children will
be able to get away or say "No" (Kolko, 1988). Finally, the effectiveness of
prevention programs for young children increases as the time, effort, and one-
on-one practice provided increase, and "booster" sessions may be essential
for maintaining effectiveness over time (Garbarino, 1988).

It is important to recognize that even the most effective sexual abuse
prevention programs do not demonstrate that children acquire all the information and skills taught. Moreover, there is no ethical way to demonstrate
that children actually use the skills they have learned in abusive situations.

Interviews with sexual abuse offenders (Conte, Wolf, & Smith, 1989) indicate that offenders are extremely sophisticated about desensitizing their young victims to touch before actually molesting them. Offenders also report typically using various kinds of threats to intimidate children. Most sex abuse prevention programs do not take these issues adequately into account, and even if they did, children involved in abusive situations could be confused and unable to use the skills they have learned.

Almost all efforts at child sexual abuse prevention have been directed toward children. Although these programs have demonstrated some effectiveness in enhancing children's skills and knowledge, they have not demonstrated a contribution to a decrease in the incidence of sexual abuse or an increase in disclosures (Wurtele & Miller-Perrin, 1992). Consequently, it is important for professionals to begin to target other aspects of the child sexual abuse phenomenon. A review of the epidemiological characteristics of child sexual abuse by Wurtele and Miller-Perrin (1992) suggests several potential targets:

1. *Potential perpetrators of sexual abuse.* For example, a recent program was designed to teach adolescents who were at risk of abusing children about the nature and causes of child sexual abuse, in addition to empathy, anger management, problem solving, decision making, and impulse control skills (Committee for Children, 1989).

2. *Sociocultural attitudes and beliefs.* It has been suggested that societal attitudes about children, male socialization, sexuality, and male–female relationships contribute to a social context that supports sexual abuse of children (Wurtele & Miller-Perrin, 1992).

3. *Mass media and pornography.* Although a direct connection between erotic portrayals of children and child sexual abuse has not been consistently documented (Murrin & Laws, 1990), it seems reasonable to assume that such films, advertising, and other media may contribute to an increased sexual interest in children and decreased inhibitions about sexual contacts with children.

To summarize, there is no evidence that sexual abuse prevention programs decrease the incidence of sexual abuse or increase the rate of disclosure. The nature of sexual abuse is such that many children are likely to find it difficult to use the knowledge and skills gained from prevention programs to protect themselves. Thus, more prevention efforts should be directed toward potential perpetrators such as high-risk adolescents, and towards societal attitudes and mass media, rather than just focusing on the potential victims. Sexual abuse prevention programs for children are most appropriately thought of as aspects of general sex education. At the same time children are learning about their bodies, it is important to teach them what is abusive behavior, how to protect themselves from abusive sexual interactions with others, including siblings and friends, and the consequences of coercing other children to engage in sexual behaviors. An important part of this education is teaching children how to be assertive and to make good decisions in the context of both sexual and social relationships. It is most important that parents be supported in providing this education from the time of birth and throughout their children's development. The nature of the information taught and the methods of teaching will vary depending on the age of the child. But even very young children can grasp simple concepts of body parts and functions, protection of their own genitalia, the rights of others to personal privacy, and the importance of telling someone when they are distressed. Although prevention programs have typically targeted preschool and elementary school-aged children, adolescents (and adults), particularly those at risk for abusing children, also would benefit from information about sexual abuse and the consequences of coercive sexual behaviors.

SUMMARY AND CONCLUSIONS

At a time when allegations of child sexual abuse are increasingly common, knowledge of normal sexual development in children is essential. Although research in this area is limited, it has important implications for professionals who are responsible for investigations of child sexual abuse. First, many of the "symptoms" thought to be indicative of child sexual abuse involve sexual behaviors that occur more or less commonly during the normal course of development. Thus, it is not necessarily valid to assume that a child who engages in behaviors such as masturbation or has a high interest in sexuality, has been abused; other alternatives must be considered. Second, coercive sexual contacts appear to be relatively common among friends and especially among siblings during childhood. Moreover, it is unlikely that these encounters will ever be discovered. Thus, it is important to teach children early in life about their own rights to privacy, as well as the rights of others, and how to resist coercive sexual interactions. Assertiveness skills may not help a child prevent an abusive sexual contact with an adult, but these skills may be very helpful in the context of peer and sibling relationships. Finally, parents need information and support from professionals to enhance their abilities to educate their children about sexuality. Sex education necessarily begins at birth and parents are the primary educators, whether or not they ever actually discuss sex with their children. Ongoing parental input is critical in preventing early sexual activity among adolescents, as well as in preventing child sexual abuse, but for those children whose families are not able or willing to provide information, school-based programs that teach commonly accepted values as well as facts are essential. Finally, parents and professionals must begin to examine critically the ways in which sexuality is portrayed in the mass media and help children place sex in the context of loving relationships.

Sexual Problems

A wide variety of sexual problems can be seen among children and adolescents, ranging from physical/anatomical abnormalities that have an impact on later psychological and social development to "public or semipublic behaviors that cause adults (usually the parents) embarrassment and concern because they are a departure from society's expectations" (Haroian, 1991, p. 432). In this chapter, we begin with a discussion of the effects of living with gay or lesbian parents. Although research has shown that children raised by homosexual parents are at no greater risk for psychological problems than those with heterosexual parents, this topic is included here because it is of increasing importance for child clinicians, especially those who deal with issues of divorce and custody. This discussion is followed by an examination of the literature on physical and behavioral sexual problems, including sexual errors of the body, gender identity disorder, precocious puberty, and sexualized behavior.

CHILDREN OF LESBIAN AND GAY PARENTS

It is estimated that between 6 and 14 million children have gay or lesbian parents. The majority of these children are born in the context of a heterosexual relationship and subsequently one parent declares his or her homosexuality. There also are, however, an increasing number of lesbian and gay couples who seek to adopt children, provide foster homes, or use artificial insemination to have children. Thus, clinicians are increasingly being asked about the impact on children of living in these "nontraditional" households.

Historically, the legal system has been hostile to gay and lesbian parents because of an assumption that growing up in such a household will have a negative impact on children's development, placing them at increased risk for aberrant psychosexual development, isolation from or rejection by peers, and other emotional or behavioral problems. Although research addressing this question is limited and primarily has been done with children of single lesbian mothers, the data overwhelmingly indicate that these children are at no greater risk for these problems than children growing up in more "traditional" households. This research is reviewed briefly here. For an in-depth review, see Patterson (1992) or contact the American Psychological Association's Committee on Lesbian and Gay Concerns.

An often expressed major concern is that children raised by homosexual parents are at high risk for abnormal sexual identity, including problems with gender identity, gender role behaviors, and sexual orientation. In a review of studies that evaluated over 300 children of gay or lesbian parents in 12 different samples, Patterson (1992) found that these children did not exhibit significant problems in any of these areas. The children were happy with the sex to which they belonged, had no wish to be members of the opposite sex, and their interests and preference for activities were no different than those of other children. Further, there was no evidence that the number of children who as adults identified themselves as gay or lesbian exceeded that expected in the population at large.

According to the Patterson (1992) review, children of gay and lesbian parents were also found to have normal relationships both with their peers and adults of both sexes. When compared with heterosexual single mothers, lesbian mothers had more adult male family friends, included more male relatives in their children's activities, and had fewer problems with their children's contact with their fathers. In fact, children living with lesbian mothers were found to have more contact with their fathers than children living with single heterosexual mothers. Further, there is no evidence to support the fear that children with homosexual parents are more vulnerable to being sexually abused either by the parent or the parent's acquaintances than children with heterosexual parents. There were no differences in the behavioral or emotional development of these two groups of children.

Not surprisingly, the quality of the relationships within the family seem to be more important than the sexual orientation of the parents in influencing children's development. For example, if the parents are able to be open about their sexual orientation and this is accepted by other significant people, the mental health of both parents and children is likely to be improved (Rand, Graham, & Rawlings, 1982). Furthermore, unless there is some reason to highlight parental sexuality (e.g., a divorced parent remarries), most children do not think of their parents as sexual beings and the significance of a sexual relationship is not fully understood until adolescence. This was recently demonstrated when the parents of a 10-year-old boy told him that they were expecting a baby. This youngster was astounded, saying, "But mother, *who* got you pregnant?"!

Children's ability to accept their parent's homosexuality is influenced by when they first learn about it. It is not surprising that children in early to middle adolescence have the most difficulty (Schulenberg, 1985). In general, we have found that the acceptance of the parent's homosexuality by significant adults in the child's life, particularly the other parent, helps the child understand and accept the parent's sexual orientation. When discussing sexual orientation with children, it is important to emphasize relationships rather than sexual behavior, per se. As with any stressful life event, it is helpful for children to have the opportunity to talk with other children who have had similar experiences. Thus, participation in groups with other children who have gay or lesbian parents can be quite helpful. A book by Rafkin (1990) shares stories by children growing up in lesbian families and another by Russ (1990) is helpful for the professional working with families where the parents are homosexual.

SEX ERRORS OF THE BODY

When a baby is born, the first information received by parents is whether the infant is a boy or a girl. This information sets in motion a chain of events and behaviors that over the course of development, will influence the child's understanding of him- or herself as masculine or feminine. For most families, the news about the sex of the child is part of a joyous occasion. For others, however, fetal development is incomplete or abnormal at birth and the sex of the child is an issue that parents and physicians must resolve. A full discussion of the physiology and anatomy of these sex errors of the body is beyond the scope of this volume, but the reader is referred to an easily understandable book, *Sex Errors of the Body and Related Syndromes: A Guide to Counseling Children, Adolescents, and Their Families* by John Money (1994). The following discussion is based on this work.

The process of sexual differentiation during fetal development follows what Money (1994) calls the Eve/Adam principle; that is, nature's first priority is to develop females. Development of males is more complex than that of females, requiring the addition of male hormone secretion to the developmental process for success. At conception, the fetus has the potential to be either male or female. It is not until about the second or third month of gestation that sex differentiation begins to occur. Money (1994) outlines the process as follows: (1) Genetic or chromosomal sex is determined at conception by the contribution of an X chromosome from the mother and either an X or Y chromosome from the father. (2) Next, undifferentiated fetal gonads develop in both male and female fetuses—testes at about 6 weeks and ovaries at about 12 weeks. (3) Between the third and fourth month of gestation, if the baby is to be a boy, the testes begin to secrete male hormones—androgen and antimullerian hormone—which prod the development of male sexual anatomy and inhibit development of female anatomy, respectively. The lack of these male hormones results in female development, regardless of the chromosomal sex of the fetus. (4) Finally, also stimulated by the secretion or lack of secretion of male hormones, differentiated external sex organs develop.

Sex errors of the body can occur at any of these stages of development. Thus, there are sex chromosomal abnormalities such as Klinefelter syndrome (which involves an extra X chromosome, 47,XXY), and Turner syndrome (involving a missing chromosome, 45,X), gonadal abnormalities such as undescended or missing testicles, and Swyer syndrome (46,XY without testicles or ovaries), fetal hormonal anomalies such as androgen insensitivity syndrome (AIS), and abnormalities of the internal and external sex organs. Each of these can result in variations of hermaphroditism or intersexuality, of which three types have been defined: (1) true hermaphroditism in which both ovarian and testicular tissue is present and external genitalia are ambiguous; (2) female hermaphroditism in which external genitalia are masculine but ovaries are present; and (3) male hermaphroditism in which external genitalia are female but female internal organs are missing or malformed. There are also abnormalities of the external genitalia that do not involve hermaphroditism such as lack of a penis (penile agenesis), a very small penis (micropenis), or insufficient or lack of vaginal orifice (vaginal atresia). Money (1994) provides detailed descriptions of the etiology and clinical manifestations of each of these abnormalities (a summary is shown in Table 2.1).

Sex errors of the body are relatively rare but are more often found in males than in females due to the greater complexity of male development. For both sexes, the extent of abnormality of the external genitalia varies but the issue of sex assignment is usually central. Because reconstruction of male external genitalia may not be very satisfactory, sex assignment often is female.

Although child clinicians should have some understanding of the etiology and specific manifestations of the various sex errors of the body, the most important issue for these professionals is how to counsel children born with sex errors and their families. Counseling typically begins at the infant's birth and continues aperiodically throughout development, involving parents, the child, and his or her siblings. Money (1994) provides some excellent suggestions for clinicians. He states that a helpful way to describe these children to parents and other family members is as having been born "sexually unfin-

Table 2.1   Sex Errors of the Body

Sex Chromosome Abnormalities

Triple X syndrome (47,XXX)	Associated with mental retardation, although many appear normal and are not detected. The more extra X chromosomes the greater the mental retardation.
Supernumerary syndrome (47,XYY)	Associated with criminality/aggression but many in normal population have this syndrome. Associated with high impulsivity which causes school/learning and behavioral problems. Average to high IQ and height over 6 ft are typical.
Klinefelter syndrome (47,XXY)	Typically diagnosed at puberty with swelling of breasts, small testicles, small penis, insufficient masculinization. Associated with sterility, low sex drive, language and reading problems. Mental retardation is seen in some.
Turner syndrome (45,X)	Short stature, missing or abnormal ovaries or testicles, female external genitalia. May have other physical anomolies. Uterus is present and menstruation may occur. Associated with a variety of learning problems, especially low nonverbal IQ. 45X/46XY is a variation which includes male or ambiguous external genitalia.

Gonadal Abnormalities

Undescended testicles	Very common and usually self-corrects at puberty. May signal some other abnormality, e.g., lack of testicles.
Swyer syndrome (46,XY)	Failure to develop either ovaries or testicles because of missing gene on short arm of Y chromosome. Fetus develops as female without ovaries because of lack of male hormone secretion. Uterus is present. Diagnosed at puberty because of lack of breast development and menstruation.

Fetal Hormonal Anomalies

Androgen insensitivity syndrome (46,XY)	A form of male hermaphroditism. Caused by defective gene on X chromosome that interferes with absorption of androgen. Testes are formed and secrete male hormones so that female internal organs do not develop. External genitalia are female because androgen is not absorbed. Breasts develop because of small amounts of estrogen secreted by testicles. Often diagnosed at puberty with lack of menstruation. Sex assignment is female. Treatment involves removal of testicles and female hormone replacement therapy.

(Continued)

Table 2.1   Sex Errors of the Body (Continued)

Fetal Hormonal Anomalies (Continued)

Persistent Mullerian duct syndrome (46,XY)	Failure to secrete or absorb antimullerian hormone which inhibits development of female organs. External genitalia are male, internal are both male and female. May be infertile. Treatment involves removal of female organs.
Congenital adrenal hyperplasia syndrome (46,XX)	A form of female hermaphroditism. Excess androgen secreted when external genitalia are formed. Results in female internal organs and male or ambiguous external organs. Masculinization continues at puberty if untreated. External genitalia unsuitable for sexual intercourse unless surgically corrected. Sex assignment is typically female and hormone treatment is lifelong.
True hermaphroditism (typically 46,XX but can be 46,XY or 46,XX/46,XY)	Thought to be caused when male determining material from Y chromosome splices onto X chromosome. Ovary on one side of body and testicle on the other. External genitalia are ambiguous. Sex assignment depends on prospects for sexual intercourse and fertility in adulthood.

Nonhermaphroditic External Anomalies

Hypospadias (46,XY)	Urinary opening is misplaced along the penis instead of at tip. May be mild or severe. Corrected surgically. Associated with undescended or missing testicles. May be caused by poorly done circumcision.
Epispadias (46,XX or 46,XY)	Malformation of urinary and/or defecatory systems. Surgical repair may result in incontinence. Male penis may be abnormal and best reassigned as female.
Micropenis (46,XY) penile agenesis	Missing or very small penis. When extreme, typically reassigned as female. Treatment involves surgical correction at birth, gender identity training, hormone therapy and surgery for vaginal construction in adolescence.
Vaginal atresia (46,XX or 46,XY))	Insufficient or lack of vaginal orifice. Can be caused by androgen insensitivity syndrome in 46,XY males or MRK syndrome in 46,XX females. Ovaries usually present but uterus and vagina are malformed. Often diagnosed at puberty with lack of menstruation.

ished.'' The focus of medical intervention is one of finishing the task that nature left unfinished. When sex reassignment is an issue, the first step in treatment is to determine what sex the child is to be. This decision should be based on multiple factors, including the child's genetic sex, the nature of internal sex organs, and most important, the external genitalia. The question should be asked, How will this child function best sexually as an adult? Open discussion with parents about the child's physical condition, the necessary medical interventions, and their feelings regarding the sex of their child is essential. Parents who are not comfortable (for whatever reason) with the assigned sex of the child will be less able to carry out the necessary but often complicated medical and behavioral recommendations. Open communication with other family members also is critical when sex reassignment is an issue. Siblings, for example, may hold the misguided belief that their sex might be reassigned as well. Moreover, grandparents and others who will be caring for the infant need to be prepared for the child's unusual appearance.

Children born with sex errors of the body need a variety of information as they grow and develop. As many parents are unable or unwilling to discuss these sensitive issues with their children, this task often falls to professionals. Information must be geared to the child's ability to understand, but should include the etiology (e.g., chromosomal or hormonal) and prognosis (e.g., prospects for fertility or sexual intercourse) specific to the child's abnormality, and basic sexuality education, including the physiology and anatomy of reproduction, as well as the psychological and sociological aspects of sexuality. These children often have difficulty with self-image and self-esteem, particularly as they approach adolescence. For some children, sexual preference and/ or gender identity may also be central issues. The nature and timing of any necessary surgery is particularly important to discuss with children and parents. Surgery to correct external and internal abnormalities can interact with issues of development such as adolescent sexual identity.

Money (1994) describes an approach called ''the parable technique'' which is designed to help open discussion with the child about sexual matters. The therapist tells a story based on the child's own experience and medical history that deals with issues likely to be important for the child, such as reconstructive genital surgery, fear of rejection, telling peers or siblings, gender issues, and so forth. The story communicates to the child that it is all right to talk about any of these difficult topics and allows for further questioning and discussion in a nonjudgmental atmosphere. Through education and support of their sexuality, children with sex errors of the body can be helped to develop along the normal continuum.

GENDER IDENTITY DISORDER

The development of an awareness of oneself as male or female and the value one places on being a member of one's sex, or gender identity, begins very early in life. Hospital personnel, parents and families typically begin to influence the development of gender identity at birth by providing blue or pink clothing and masculine or feminine names depending on the child's physical sex. Same-sex preferences typically are reflected in children's behavior (e.g., choice of toys, games, playmates, clothing) by the age of 2 years, and most children have developed at least a partial understanding of the concept of gender identity by 2 to 3 years (Gordon et al., 1990a; Rutter, 1970). Boys appear to develop a same-sex preference earlier and more consistently than do girls (Rutter, 1975), probably reflecting differential societal attitudes toward sex-typed behaviors for boys and girls. A full understanding of gender roles (the behaviors, attitudes, and traits designated by society as male or female at any given time) typically develops between 3 and 7 years, although aspects of sex-typed behaviors are seen earlier (e.g., boys play with cars and trucks and girls play with dolls). It is not clear whether gender identity precedes gender-typed behavior ("I am a girl therefore I want to do girl things" [Zucker & Green, 1992, p. 110]) or vice versa ("I like to do girl things therefore I must be a girl" [Zucker & Green, 1992, p. 110]). There is probably a reciprocal interaction between the two early in life, although there may be a predisposition to organize information along gender lines that first influences behavior and later influences how children understand the social world (Zucker & Green, 1992).

Whatever the developmental process, most children engage in behaviors and hold preferences that are consistent with their physical gender beginning in the preschool years. For some children, however, there is a significant incongruity between their biological sex and preferred gender. These children express a firm desire to be (or a belief that they are) of the opposite sex, and are preoccupied with activities that are strongly associated with the opposite sex. They are different from children who are simply "tomboys" or "sissies," and often receive a diagnosis of Gender Identity Disorder (GID).

Diagnostic Issues

In the fourth edition of the *Diagnostic and Statistical Manual of Mental Disorders* (DSM-IV; American Psychiatric Association, 1994) the diagnostic criteria for GID include two central features: (1) strong and persistent cross-gender identification as manifested in a desire to be or belief that one is the opposite sex, and preferences for stereotypical cross-gender clothing, activities, or playmates and roles in fantasy or make-believe play; and (2) persistent discomfort with one's own sex as manifested in aversion to one's own genitalia, or sex-typed behavior, activities, or clothing. It is important to note that the first criteria, to some extent, is dependent on age; older children are less likely to state a wish to be or believe that they are the opposite sex (Zucker, 1990a), probably because they are more aware of social stigmatization.

Gender Identity Disorder is a relatively rare disorder. In a nonclinical sample, Achenbach and Edelbrock (1981) found that 0 to 2% of boys and 2 to 5% of girls were reported by their parents to express a wish to be the opposite sex, but it is not known how many of these children would fulfill all the criteria for a DSM-IV diagnosis of GID. Prevalence rates for GID have been estimated to be 1 in 24,000 to 37,000 for males and 1 in 103,000 to 150,000 for females, with higher rates for a clinical sample (1–16% of boys and 6–8% of girls) (Meyer-Bahlburg, 1985). Referral rates are much higher for boys than girls (5.25 to 1), raising the question of whether the prevalence of GID is actually higher for boys than for girls. It may be that boys are more vulnerable to GID because masculine development is dependent on prenatal androgen secretion whereas feminine development occurs in the absence of prenatal androgens (Money & Ehrhardt, 1972). Alternatively, the higher refer-ral rates for boys may be due to the fact that society has less tolerance for cross-gender behavior in boys. Girls may have to show more severe and persistant cross-gender preference before their parents become concerned enough to seek professional help.

Although a diagnosis of GID is rare, cross-gender behavior in young children is quite common, and parents often request assistance in dealing with it. In Achenbach and Edelbrock's (1981) normal sample, 3 to 6% of boys and 10 to 12% of girls were reported to engage in behavior typical of the opposite sex. Thus, an important issue for assessment is the differentiation of clinically significant cross-gender behavior from that which is seen in normally devel-oping children. Zucker and Green (1992) provide guidelines for making this important distinction. They state that although girls who are considered to be "tomboys" engage in much male sex-typed behavior, they are not likely to be *intensely* unhappy about being girls or having female anatomy. Moreover, these girls are not *intensely* opposed to wearing feminine clothing for certain functions. Likewise, boys who might be labeled "sissies," may not like to participate in typically masculine activities but do not wish to be female.

Symptoms of GID appear to be age-dependent, at least for boys; little is known about the course of the disorder in girls. Cross-gender behavior and explicit statements about wishing to be the opposite sex decrease with age, probably because of the social stigma associated with these behaviors. Thus, few boys who are diagnosed with GID in childhood will continue to meet the DSM-IV criteria in adolescence or adulthood (American Psychiatric Association, 1994). Adolescent boys and girls who continue to have persistent problems with gender identity are at high risk for transsexualism (i.e., individuals who desire a sex change) (Rekers, 1991; Zucker & Green, 1992).

Because the symptoms of GID are age-dependent, Zucker and Green (1992) argue for a comprehensive assessment for all children, and most especially adolescents, who are suspected of having gender identity problems. The assessment should include objective as well as projective measures, to ensure that covert wishes or fantasies about being the opposite sex are noted even when little overt cross-gender behavior is evident.

Another reason for the necessity of a comprehensive assessment is that GID often occurs with other forms of psychopathology, particularly internalizing disorders. Coates and Person (1985), for example, found high rates of separation anxiety, peer rejection, and depression (including some children with suicide attempts or suicidal ideation) in their sample of children with GID. Older children with GID (particularly adolescents) appear to have higher rates of comorbid psychopathology than do younger children (Zucker, 1990b), which may reflect the cumulative effects of peer rejection and social isolation that almost inevitably accompany GID.

Etiology

Zucker and Green (1992) summarize the research related to various theories about the etiology of GID. They conclude that there is some evidence that biological factors, particularly prenatal hormone secretion, may predispose children to problems with gender identity. Variations in prenatal hormone exposure (i.e., increases or decreases in androgens) have been shown to influence later behavior in both animals and humans (Money & Ehrhardt, 1972). Female fetuses exposed to androgens prenatally exhibit behaviors more typical of males after birth, whereas male fetuses which are not exposed to sufficient levels of androgens exhibit more typically feminine behaviors. The causes of variations in hormone secretion during pregnancy are not well understood. In rats prenatal maternal stress has been linked with decreased androgen secretion and later demasculinized behavior in the male offspring (Ward, 1984). To date, however, there have been no definitive studies that replicate this particular phenomenon in humans.

Further evidence for a biological contribution to GID is found in studies that indicate that boys with GID are more physically attractive than control boys (Green, 1987). Stoller (1975) speculates that some parents might be more likely to encourage feminine behavior if their sons are particularly attractive. Added to these data are those of Gewirtz, Weber, and Nogueras (1990, cited in Zucker & Green, 1992) who demonstrated that physical facial features of infants were correlated with adults' ability to predict the sex of the infants. Thus, it may be that certain physical characteristics, such as facial features, elicit behavior from adults that reinforces feminine or masculine behavior independent of the child's physical gender.

Evidence for the role of the social environment in GID is found in studies that show successful formation of gender identity in children born with ambiguous genitalia and assigned to one sex or another shortly after birth (Money, Devore, & Norman, 1986, 1987; Quattrin, Aronica, & Mazur, 1990). Other research demonstrates higher rates of parental and family dysfunction for children with GID than for controls (see for example, Marantz & Coates, 1991), Moreover, clinical experience indicates that parents of children with GID often respond neutrally or positively to their children's early cross-gender behavior, thus potentially increasing this behavior through differential reinforcement (Zucker & Green, 1992).

Taken together, research on the etiology of GID suggests that this disorder probably results from an interaction between biological and environmental factors. Money and Russo (1979) suggest that fetal sex hormones influence brain development which subsequently mediates behavior. This process creates a predisposition to behave as a male or female. The social environment then functions to reinforce or discourage cross- or same-gender behavior and identification. This view suggests that the occurrence of other forms of psychopathology with gender disturbances may be the result of the social consequences (peer rejection, social isolation, and poor self-esteem) of engaging in cross-gender behavior.

Long-Term Prognosis

Although GID is a relatively rare disorder, the significance of the disorder recently has been clearly demonstrated, at least for boys. Too few girls have been followed prospectively to have a clear picture of their outcomes, but, based on retrospective studies, Rekers (1991) argues that childhood gender disturbances among girls can lead to homosexuality or transsexualism in adulthood. For boys, a very strong association between gender disturbances in childhood and later homosexuality has been demonstrated in both retrospective and prospective research (Green, 1985; Zucker 1990a; Zucker & Green, 1992). For instance, adult homosexuals consistently recall more cross-gender behavior in childhood than do heterosexuals (e.g., Bell, Weinberg, & Hammer-smith, 1981; Rekers & Lovaas, 1974; Whitam & Mathy, 1986). Prospective work indicates that a substantial majority (estimates range from 0 to 100%, with longer follow-up resulting in larger percentages; Zucker, 1990a) of boys with GID have a homosexual or bisexual orientation as adults (e.g., Green, 1987; Money & Russo, 1979). Thus, cross-gender identity may be a precursor of homosexuality. Alternatively, cross-gender identity and homosexuality may be two different manifestations of the same underlying phenomenon, with cross-gender behavior more salient early in development and homosexual behavior seen later. This latter theory is supported by the fact that deviant gender identity for most boys with GID normalizes with development and by the fact that most adult homosexuals do not demonstrate gender identity or gender role problems as adults (Zucker & Green, 1992). The reason why gender identity appears to normalize with development is not yet clear. It may be, however, that gender identity problems are resolved through the process of determining one's sexual orientation.

It would be reasonable to expect a similar strong association between GID and transsexualism (adults who have persistent gender identity problems and wish to undergo sex reassignment); however, research indicates a some-what different picture. Although retrospective studies show that almost all adult transsexuals (both male and female) recall cross-gender behavior as children (e.g., Blanchard, Clemmensen, & Steiner, 1987), prospective studies of children with GID indicate that very few become transsexuals as adults (Green, 1987; Money & Russo, 1979). Zucker and Green (1992) propose three explanations for these findings: (1) Base rates for transsexualism are so low that large numbers of childhood GID cases would be needed to find any adult transsexuals. (2) Transsexuals come from families in which cross-gender behavior is condoned and thus these children never come to the attention of mental health or research professionals. (3) Assessment for research studies and subsequent treatment may alter the natural course of GID, thus preventing the development of transsexualism.

Transvestism (cross-dressing for purposes of sexual arousal) does not appear to be related to GID, and in fact, the clinical picture for this disorder is quite different than that of GID. Transvestites typically do not have gender problems as children and are usually quite securely masculine as adults. Moreover, they clearly demonstrate masculine gender roles (Blanchard, 1990). The function of cross-dressing appears to distinguish potential transvestitism from GID. Cross-dressing among gender disturbed boys is done for the purpose of enhancing their identification with the opposite sex (typically employing outer clothing) as opposed to a soothing or erotic function (typically involving female underwear) for transvestism (Zucker & Green, 1992).

To summarize, a strong association between cross-gender disturbances in children and homosexual behavior in adults has been clearly demonstrated. The association is not as strong for transsexualism and there appears to be little relationship between transvestism and GID.

── **Treatment**

Treatment of gender problems in children has generated a considerable amount of controversy. One view argues that treatment reinforces a sexist view of childrearing (Zucker, 1990c) and therefore it is inappropriate to try to change the child's discordant gender identity. According to this view, rigid sex-typed behavior is undesirable and it would be more appropriate to change societal attitudes about which behaviors are labeled as "deviant." This, in turn, might decrease the extent to which other psychopathology accompanies gender disturbances (Winkler, 1977). Others have questioned the ethics of treating GID in the attempt to prevent homosexuality (although it is not clear that treatment is effective in this regard), and argue that the treatment could, in effect, cause more harm than good by focusing on the idea that homosexuality is undesirable (Green, 1987).

An alternative view proposes that early treatment of GID could at least alleviate the peer relationship and self-esteem problems that accompany the disorder, and may be effective in resolving the gender identity disturbance (Rekers, Kilgus, & Rosen, 1990; Zucker, 1990c). This view supports early intervention to eliminate cross-gender behaviors and to replace them with behaviors that are consistent with the child's physical sex. This approach might speed up the natural developmental process of cross-gender behavior (i.e., a decrease with age) and prevent the development of other forms of psychopathology that typically result from peer rejection.

A third approach would be to focus treatment on acknowledging and affirming the child's cross-gender preference and then helping the child learn how to express this preference in a manner that allows for good peer relations while maintaining a positive self-image. According to this view, cross-gender behaviors are only seen as problematic in reference to where and when they are expressed.

Given that the research on treatment of children born with ambiguous sex organs indicates that gender identity can be successfully taught, at least early in life (e.g., Money et al., 1986; Money & Norman, 1987; Quattrin et al., 1990), it would seem reasonable for clinicians to intervene to replace cross-gender with same-gender behavior in preschool children. Since gender identity and gender roles are firmly established by age 7, intervention with the goal of changing cross-gender identity is less likely to be effective after this age. Therefore, for preadolescent children whose gender identity is persistently of the opposite sex, an approach that helps them accept themselves as they are while recognizing and adapting to societal norms may be appropriate.

A behavioral approach to treatment of GID in children is most common. This approach assumes that cross-gender behavior is learned and therefore can be changed by manipulating the consequences for cross- and same-gender behavior (Meyer-Bahlburg, 1985; Zucker, 1990c). A behavioral approach involves providing opportunities and positive reinforcement for engaging in gender-appropriate behavior and choosing gender-appropriate games and toys, giving verbal feedback about appropriate and inappropriate gender behavior, and extinguishing cross-gender behavior by ignoring it (Rekers & Lovaas, 1974; Schaefer & Millman, 1981). Zucker (1990c) suggests "that parents disallow cross-dressing, discourage cross-gender roleplay and fantasy play, restrict playing with cross-sex toys, tell the child that they value him as a boy (or her as a girl), encourage same sex peer relations, and help the child engage in more sex appropriate or neutral activities" (p.38). For example, the clinician might instruct the parents of a 4-year-old girl who insists on only playing the male role in make-believe play to reply: "This time I want to play the prince and you play Cinderella." If the child persists, the parent can be instructed to say that he or she does not want to play that game today.

Self-esteem enhancement that is focused on gender related issues is also an important component of treatment in most cases of GID (Pope, McHale, & Craighead, 1988). For example, the clinician can instruct parents to describe positively the specific gender related attributes of the child ("You are such a strong young man. I really appreciate your carrying in the groceries. You are getting to be just like your Dad.")

Parental involvement is essential to the success of treatment, both to provide them with insight as to their contribution to the problem (if any) and so they can assist with the treatment program. Parents can contribute by ensuring that the program is implemented consistently across settings and people. However, treatment of any accompanying parental or family psychopathology would be essential to maximize the effectiveness of the treatment program.

Although clinicians should be alert to the possibility of GID in children referred for cross-gender behavior, they should also be aware that current research supports the idea that healthy personality development depends in part on both masculine *and* feminine characteristics. Children who engage in cross-sex behavior, but are entirely comfortable with their own gender, may in fact be exhibiting quite adaptive behavior. Nonetheless, treatment is clearly indicated for those children who have an intense and persistent desire to be the opposite sex. Although such treatment may not prevent homosexuality, it will at least ensure that the child is better adjusted and more accepting of him- or herself.

DELAYED OR PRECOCIOUS PUBERTY

The onset of puberty is a time of dramatic physical changes. Along with large increases in height and weight and the development of secondary sex characteristics, adolescents often experience increases in activity level and emotional lability as a function of changes within their endrocrine systems (Rekers, 1991). It should not be surprising that this period of rapid development is associated with adjustment problems in a number of areas, such as self-image, body image, peer relations, and parental relations, even among normally developing teens (Brooks-Gunn & Warren, 1988).

The age at which children normally reach puberty, ranges from 10 to 16 years among girls and 11 to 16 years among boys. Puberty is considered to be precocious or delayed if it occurs outside this normal range; that is, before age 9 in girls and age 10 in boys (Sonis et al., 1986) and after age 16 for both sexes. The age at which puberty is reached appears to have a significant impact on adjustment, although the problems experienced as a result of delayed or precocious puberty are different for boys and girls (Rutter, 1970; Rutter & Rutter, 1993). Adolescents who are early or late maturing are at risk for problems with peer acceptance, but boys tend to suffer more from delayed puberty while girls experience more problems associated with early or precocious puberty.

Precocious puberty is caused by increased levels of sex steroids, which can have a variety of etiologies including: (1) central nervous system lesions, such as hydrocephalus; (2) as part of an identified syndrome, such as neurofibromatosis; (3) genetic disorders; or (4) a premature signal from the hypothalmic–pituitary biological clock (Money, 1994; Sonis et al., 1986; Tomono, Maki, Ito, & Nakada, 1983). Regardless of its cause, the early onset of puberty clearly interacts with other social and psychological factors in ways that have the potential to alter a child's developmental course. For boys, distinct advantages come with early maturation. Increases in height and weight, for example, enhance boys' abilities to compete in athletics. As a result, early maturing boys often receive more positive feedback from adults and may be considered more attractive by their peers. These advantages result in higher self-esteem, greater self-confidence and social maturity (Rekers, 1991). In contrast, boys who mature late tend to be less popular, less confident, and more withdrawn, and these effects may persist into adulthood (Rutter, 1970).

For girls, the impact of the timing of puberty is quite different from the impact for boys. Late maturing girls are more in step with the boys in their peer groups and thus are not likely to experience significant adjustment problems associated with onset of puberty. In contrast, girls who mature very early are at risk for a number of behavior problems, both internalizing and externalizing. Sonis et al. (1986) found that girls with precocious puberty exhibited 10 times more behavior problems in the areas of social withdrawal, depression, aggression, and social competence than did a group of matched controls. Although some girls who mature early may withdraw and consequently become less popular among their peer group (Rekers, 1991), others have been shown to engage in a range of precocious sexual behaviors, including sexual intercourse (Meyer-Bahlburg et al., 1985). The reason for this early sexual behavior may be that girls who mature early appear older than their peers and may be exposed to sexual advances that are not appropriate for their chronological age and level of social and emotional development.

Treatment of precocious or delayed puberty should include a thorough medical evaluation to determine the cause and rule out dangerous conditions (e.g., a brain tumor). Hormonal therapy may be indicated to slow down or stop the process of puberty and allow for normal bone growth when onset is exceedingly premature, or to precipitate the onset of puberty when it is quite delayed (Money, 1994). Psychological intervention is likely to involve issues of self-esteem and social relations. Rekers (1991) suggests that group treatment with other children who are late or early to mature can focus on empathy and social skills. The clinician can help parents to understand the potential lability in the child's moods and they can be encouraged to provide the child with opportunities for age appropriate activities. Finally, sex education with an emphasis on the bodily changes that are occurring and the potential for sexual exploitation is essential for these children.

OVERSEXUALIZED AND SEXUALLY AGGRESSIVE BEHAVIOR

Although all children display interest and curiosity about sexuality at various times during their development, some appear to be overly focused and preoccupied with sexual matters beyond what is expected for their age. These children have variously been labeled as oversexualized, child perpetrators, sexually aggressive, or child offenders. Their behavior may vary a great deal, ranging from compulsive, public masturbation to coercive or aggressive sexual interactions with other children. For the most part, the behavior is unresponsive to parental limit setting, interferes with other age appropriate activities, and may be indicative of serious psychopathology.

Sexualized Behavior

Sexualized behavior is thought to be associated with sexual abuse, and indeed, many sexual behaviors (e.g., asks to engage in sex acts, puts mouth on sex parts, masturbates with objects, etc.) have been shown to occur more frequently among children who have been sexually abused than in those who have not (Friedrich et al., 1992). But not all children who exhibit these types of behavior have been sexually abused, and conversely, many children who have been abused do not exhibit sexualized behavior. Healy, Fitzpatrick, and Fitzgerald (1991), for example, describe two girls, aged 9 and 10 years, who were thought to have been abused because they were engaging in compulsive sexual behavior (including masturbation, sexual contact with younger children, and obsessive thoughts about sexual matters). Through careful assessment (including interviews with the children and parents and psychological testing), both girls were determined not to have been abused and were successfully treated using a cognitive–behavioral approach.

Sexualized behavior can involve more than one participant or can consist of solitary behaviors that are engaged in excessively or in public. Lucy Berliner (cited in Friedrich, 1990) has described three levels of sexualized behavior: (1) coercive sexual behavior where physical force, verbal threats, or social coercion are used to gain another child's compliance; (2) developmentally precocious sexual behavior, such as noncoercive attempted or completed intercourse; and (3) inappropriate sexual behavior including persistent, public masturbation, sexualization of nonsexual situations, or repeatedly exhibiting genitalia. Behaviors at levels two and three are not necessarily considered indicators of psychopathology, but would suggest the need for evaluation. They would be considered serious if they were found to be frequent, persistent, or pervasive across many situations, interfere with the child's development, or be accompanied by other disturbed behavior (Friedrich, 1990).

Excessive masturbation is a very common type of sexualized behavior and the question of when it is abnormal among children is central. Masturbation is seen by most sexologists to be an important developmental step in becoming reliably orgasmic in adult partner sex (Haroian, 1991). Furthermore, it is viewed by many as a viable sexual activity throughout the lifespan. Because it is inherently pleasurable, the key clinical questions regarding masturbation among children are not *why* they masturbate, but *how much* and *where* masturbation occurs. Although there is a great deal of variation, boys are generally observed to masturbate earlier and more frequently than girls. Boys also are more likely to masturbate socially, in groups of two or more, while girls tend to engage in this behavior alone. Further, the frequency of masturbation appears to increase with age, reaching a peak at or just before puberty (Martinson, 1981).

Whether or not masturbation constitutes a "problem" is largely a function of family, societal, and cultural attitudes. A case example cited in Routh and Schroeder (1981, p. 387) illustrates this issue. The mother of a 4-year-old girl wanted advice on how to stop her daughter from masturbating while she watched TV. When asked why she was concerned about her child's masturbation, the mother stated "Because my mother-in-law is coming to visit next week!" Clearly, this mother was not worried about her child's masturbation per se, but was concerned about the social implications of the behavior for the child and family. Like most other children, this child had to learn to manage personal needs and behaviors in socially acceptable ways.

Sexualized behavior that occurs to the extent that it interferes with other age-appropriate activities may be a warning signal that a child has other problems. For instance, children who have been sexually abused often masturbate excessively. But all children who masturbate, even to excess, have not been sexually abused. Nonetheless, children who engage in excessive sexualized behaviors often have other problems such as being withdrawn, having conduct disorders, or coming from a poor home environment (Gundersen et al.,1981). Thus, the clinician needs to make a comprehensive assessment of these children and their families. This assessment should cover the child's psychological/emotional status, the home situation, and a review of the child's daily routines, including interactions with children and adults in the extended family and community. The possibility of sexual abuse should be explored, but, if possible, without raising unnecessary concerns. Problems discovered in any of the assessed areas would need to be addressed before treating the sexual behaviors themselves. Indeed as these other problems are treated, the sexual behavior may cease to be a problem.

Because sexual behaviors (especially masturbation) may be inherently pleasurable, they may continue to be a problem even after successful treatment of associated problems. For these children, the clinician may find that a behavioral approach is relatively simple and effective in eliminating the problem. Using masturbation as an example, a first step is to identify times and places when the child is most likely to masturbate and the consequences of the behavior. The child can then be reinforced for engaging in behaviors that are incompatible with masturbation (playing with or holding a toy or other object) at these times and while in public places. The idea that masturbation is all right in private is easily understood even by very young children ("I know it feels good to touch your penis/vulva, but you are only allowed to do that in your bedroom."). In addition to teaching alternative behaviors, reinforcement can be provided for increasing amounts of time not spent masturbating.

Sexualized behavior that is associated with a history of sexual abuse is considered "reactive" to the abuse and is taken as an indication that the child has not resolved the abuse experience. Treatment for these children must include attention to other issues related to sexual abuse as well as teaching the child more appropriate sexual behavior (for further discussion see Chapter 5, this volume).

Preadolescent Sexual Aggression

Sexually aggressive behaviors among preadolescents are never normal, typically reflect significant psychopathology in the child and/or family, and always warrant careful assessment and treatment by the clinician. Sexually aggressive behavior tends to be part of a larger picture of conduct problems (Friedrich, 1990), and children who engage in sexually aggressive behavior often must be thought of simultaneously as both victims and perpetrators, as it is common for them to have a history of sexual abuse. The clinical picture for children who engage in sexually aggressive behavior appears to vary depending on age (sexually aggressive behavior among adolescents is discussed in the next section) and gender. For instance, a history of sexual abuse has been found in almost all cases of sexually aggressive behavior in preadolescent girls (Johnson, 1989). These girls can be distinguished from others who have been abused but do not engage in sexually aggressive behaviors in that they have been more severely and frequently abused, have a close relationship to the perpetrator, and tend to come from very dysfunctional families who have not provided support following disclosure of the abuse (Johnson, 1989).

In contrast to girls, preadolescent boys who engage in sexually aggressive behavior may or may not have a history of sexual abuse. In a sample of 47 sexually aggressive boys, aged 4 to 13 years, reported by Johnson (1988), for example, only 49% were found to have been sexually abused and 19% were physically abused. However, most of the boys had significant school/learning and peer relationship problems, and not surprisingly, almost all came from highly dysfunctional families.

Treatment of children who engage in sexually aggressive behaviors is very complex and must necessarily be multifaceted, involving individual, group, and family intervention. The clinician can easily be overwhelmed by these difficult cases, but Friedrich (1990) suggests that a good place to start treatment is with a careful analysis of the needs and issues of the individual child and family. These can then be prioritized and treatment planned to deal with each in turn. Among the issues that are likely to be important for the clinician to deal with are those related to the child's experience of sexual abuse (see Chapter 5, this volume), controlling the child's own abusive sexual behavior, and parental management of the child's conduct disordered behavior.

Friedrich (1990) notes that individual therapy for sexually aggressive youngsters is not likely to be successful unless:

1	Ongoing support of the child is provided by a primary parent figure.
2	A sense of safety has been or is being established for the child to protect against future victimization.
3	The therapy with the child is occurring concurrently with therapy that is creating systems change and the nonabusing parent is having regular contact with the therapist.
4	The therapist is skillful, goal-oriented, conceptually clear, and willing to be directive in a supportive context.
5	The child is able to communicate regarding the abuse and can tolerate the intensity of the therapy process. (Friedrich, 1990, p. 132)

Because of the cooccurrence of sexual aggression and conduct disorder, the approach outlined by Patterson, Reid, Jones, and Conger (1975) for delinquent and aggressive youth would be an appropriate model to help parents gain better control over their child's sexual and nonsexual aggressive behaviors. This approach assumes that aggressive behavior (including sexual aggression) is learned and involves teaching parents to use a systematic system of rewards (tokens) and punishments (removal of tokens and time out) for appropriate and inappropriate behaviors. Excellent detailed descriptions of other treatment approaches for sexually aggressive children are provided by Friedrich (1990) and Gil and Johnson (1993).

Adolescent Sexual Offenders

Although adolescents are known to engage in a variety of sexual offenses, this section will focus on boys who molest children. Very little is known about adolescent girls who engage in sexually aggressive behaviors. This may be due to the fact that they rarely come to the attention of mental health or law enforcement professionals either because their numbers are very small (some estimate that over 95% of adolescent sex offenders are male; Davis & Leitenberg, 1987) or because of societal biases about male and female sexual roles. It also is possible that the sexual acting out of girls occurs in the form of promiscuity with peers rather than with younger children.

In contrast, adolescent male sexual offenders have been widely studied and are recognized to be a serious problem. During 1981, for example, adolescents accounted for 20% of the arrests for sexual offenses in the United States (Brown, Flanagan, & McLeod, 1984). Further, it has been estimated that adolescent males are responsible for up to 50% of child sexual abuse cases, and it is suspected that this may underrepresent the actual incidence because of a reluctance to report these young offenders (Davis & Leitenberg, 1987; Kempton & Forehand, 1992). The victims of adolescent sex offenders are most likely to be younger children; it is estimated that over 60% are under 12 years of age and over 40% of these are younger than 6 (Fehrenbach, Smith, Monastersky, & Deisher, 1986). Rates of repeated offenses also are very high and may be predicted by whether the initial offense was pleasurable, the consequences the offender experienced, the extent to which the offender lacks social skills, and whether the deviant behavior was reinforced by masturbation or fantasy (Becker, 1988).

Research on the nature of the assaults committed by adolescents against children indicates that up to two-thirds involve indecent liberties versus rape or attempted rape which account for about one-quarter of the offenses. In contrast to data for adult perpetrators of child sexual abuse, the majority of the victims of adolescents are male, with estimates ranging from 45 to 63% (Davis & Leitenberg, 1987). Similar to younger sexually aggressive males, not all adolescents who molest children have a history of sexual abuse; estimates range from 20 to 60%, with older boys and adult male abusers more likely to have been sexually abused than younger boys (Becker, Kaplan, & Tenke, 1992; Katz, 1990).

In an effort to understand the unique characteristics of adolescents who commit sexual offences, O'Brien and Bera (1986) have identified three categories of adolescent offenders: (1) the naive experimenter—an adolescent who has little sexual experience or knowledge and engages in a few isolated incidences of sexual contact with younger children; (2) the undersocialized child exploiter—a socially isolated adolescent who uses manipulation, trickery, or rewards to entice a child to engage in sexual activity. This type of offender may be motivated by an attempt to increase self-esteem; and (3) the pseudo-socialized child exploiter—an older adolescent with good social skills but who lacks meaningful peer relations. Sexual behavior is typically highly rationalized and the offender shows little remorse.

Although the clinical utility of these categories has yet to be demonstrated, it seems clear that personality variables play an important role in the deviant sexual behavior of these older children. There is some consensus that youngsters who commit sexual offenses are characteristically socially isolated, and have significant school/learning problems and psychopathology including both internalizing and externalizing disorders (Awad & Saunders, 1989; Katz, 1990). Unfortunately, there have been few studies that have employed adequate control groups, so it is not yet possible to determine whether these characteristics differentiate adolescents who commit sexual offenses from those who commit nonsexual offenses.

Since adolescent boys who molest children are a diverse group, treatment must be preceded by careful assessment of the individual and his family. The clinician should determine the nature of the sexual offense, the precipitating factors, and the sexual history of the adolescent and members of his immediate family (Gilby, Wolf, & Goldberg, 1989). The clinician should assess the youngster's intellectual, social, and personality functioning. If possible, there should be an evaluation of sexual arousal patterns since these appear to differentiate sex offenders from nonsex offenders as well as whether preferred victim is a younger child or a peer (Gilby et al., 1989).

Davis and Leitenberg (1987) suggest that the treatment issues that should be considered by the clinician should include: (1) accepting responsibility for the sexual offense; (2) increasing recognition of the impact of the abuse on the victim; (3) gaining insight into the motives that led to the abuse; (4) dealing with the adolescent's own experience of sexual abuse, if this has occurred; (5) sex education; (6) cognitive restructuring with regard to beliefs and myths about sexuality; (7) social skills training with a focus on dating relationships; (8) training in assertiveness skills and anger control; (9) techniques to eliminate deviant arousal patterns; and (10) family therapy to promote effective parenting. The reader also is referred to Sgroi (1989) for a description of other approaches.

Coercive Sexuality among Adolescents

Coercive sexuality among peers during adolescence also is a significant problem. A large number of girls report some unwanted sexual contact within the context of dating relationships, and many boys report they have used coercion to gain sexual contact. Various studies estimate that from 50 to 80% of girls have experienced some form of unwanted sexual contact, with 10 to 30% reporting unwanted attempted or completed intercourse (Craig, 1990). Furthermore, 15 to 25% of boys indicate that they have coerced a girl to engage in sexual intercourse against her will (Craig, 1990), and when a broad definition is used (including unwanted kissing) over 57% of college men admit to coerced sexual activity (Muehlenhard & Linton, 1987)!

Girls who experience coerced sex within a dating relationship are at risk for a number of psychological problems, including depression, self-blame, somatic symptoms, posttraumatic stress disorder and relationship problems, that can have long-term consequences. Despite this, it is likely that many girls who experience coerced sex do not seek treatment because of their own and society's tendency to "blame the victim."

Considerable research has been devoted to determining characteristics that distinguish sexually coercive males from those who are noncoercive. Craig (1990) summarizes this work:

> Sexually coercive males appear to be more aggressive, hold beliefs that relationships with women are adversarial in nature, and are supportive of rape myths and stereotypical ideas about sex roles. They tend to be more sexually experienced, but less sexually satisfied than noncoercive men, and have a family history of violence. Peer approval also plays a role, where sex is emphasized as a status symbol. Sexually coercive men are also more sexually aroused by the use of force. (Craig, 1990, p. 411)

Further, sexually coercive boys actively create dating situations in which sexual contact is likely to occur, and misperceive girls' behavior as provocative or insincere. Alcohol or other forms of intoxication are highly likely to be involved in these coercive situations (Muehlenhard & Linton, 1987).

It is not clear whether boys who engage in coercive sex within dating relationships are from the same population of teenagers who are arrested for sex offenses. It is possible that individuals in both groups represent a continuum of coercive behaviors with juvenile sex offenders engaging in more serious sexual behaviors that bring them to the attention of law enforcement agencies. It may also be the case that one or more subtypes of juvenile sex offenders may represent the extreme of those boys who engage in coercive sex in dating relationships. O'Brien and Bera (1986), for example, propose seven categories of juvenile sex offenders, one of which is called "sexual aggressive." This category includes boys who engage in coercive sexual behavior in dating relationships. These youngsters are described as having good social skills but poor impulse control. Moreover, they are likely to abuse alcohol and/or other chemicals and engage in other antisocial behaviors. The motivation for coerced sex for these youngsters is to experience personal power and/or to humiliate the victim.

Although many adolescent boys who engage in coercive sex with peers may never come to the attention of mental health professionals (i.e., their behavior is never reported by the victims), intervention for more severe cases is important because recidivism rates are so high and these youngsters are at high risk for becoming adult sexual offenders. Treatment in these cases often consists of referral to a residential sex offender program. It also seems important to attempt to prevent coercive sex in dating relationships by including this topic in sex education programs for school-aged children and adolescents. Information should be presented that describes how boys and girls perceive social situations and behaviors differently (i.e., boys tend to have a more sexualized perception of interpersonal relations and social cues than do girls) (Craig, 1990). Further, role plays can help teenagers avoid sexual conflict and exploitive situations.

SUMMARY

Children can evidence a wide variety of sexual problems all of which have the potential to impact on social and emotional development and well-being. Although physical sexual problems are relatively rare, child clinicians, especially those who work in primary health care settings, have an important role to play in helping parents and children understand and cope with the nature, course, and psychological implications of these disorders. On the other hand, questions about children's gender specific behaviors, the effects growing up with gay or lesbian parents, and sexualized behavior are increasingly being asked of child clinicians. Fortunately, empirical work in these areas provides clear guidelines for differentiating children who have clinically significant problems from those who do not and for determining effective approaches to treatment. It is particularly important that the clinician not over- or underreact when a child presents with oversexualized behavior. Sexualized behavior is not necessarily an indication that a child has been sexually abused, although there is a strong association between the two. Careful assessment is critical in understanding the etiology and seriousness of the behavior and determining a plan for intervention. In some cases, treatment may be as simple as helping the child and parents better understand and manage the behavior. In cases involving coercive sex, however, treatment may be complex, lengthy, and difficult. However, the need for intervention prior to adolescence is indicated by the possibility that similar developmental pathways exist for those who molest children and those who engage in coercive sex with peers.

Understanding Child Sexual Abuse

The sexual abuse of children has become an enormous concern for parents and professionals. The professional literature on this topic is overwhelmingly large and diverse, ranging from clinical case studies to empirical research to comprehensive review papers. In this chapter, we have tried to condense this large volume of work and focus on issues that we view as central to understanding child sexual abuse. Thus, this chapter provides a *brief* overview of definitional issues, prevalence, and characteristics of sexual abuse of boys and girls, characteristics of perpetrators, the long- and short-term effects of sexual abuse and factors that mediate these effects, issues of hidden (or repressed) memories of childhood sexual abuse, and finally, issues regarding sexual abuse in day care settings.

DEFINITIONAL ISSUES

There is not yet a commonly agreed upon definition of child sexual abuse, yet definitional issues are important in determining whether abuse has occurred in individual cases. Most definitions typically include the notions of behavior that is sexually motivated (i.e., provides sexual gratification), and an age differential between the participants (usually about 5 years). Definitions of sexual abuse may vary in whether they include behaviors that do *not* involve physical contact (e.g., exposing oneself or observing others nude), as well as those involving physical contact of various levels of intensity (e.g., touching or fondling versus vaginal, anal, or oral penetration).

The clinician should be aware that societal attitudes toward sexual contact between children and adults will necessarily influence the behaviors that are defined as sexually abusive. Perhaps because of the current concern with sexual abuse and the attention it has gotten in the mass media, there is a tendency on the part of parents and professionals to overinterpret as sexual abuse many relatively innocent encounters between adults and children that are not sexually motivated (e.g., applying ointment to the genital area or taking showers together). Similarly, children who have been exposed to sexual abuse prevention programs may be overly sensitive to innocent, incidential contact with adults such as accidentally brushing against the breasts or genitalia during a game or while being hugged, and report this behavior as abusive.

Clearly, clinicians must proceed cautiously in deciding what behaviors constitute sexual abuse. Indeed, in some cases, the events experienced by children that are labeled "sexually abusive" are far less stressful for the child than the response of the professional community and the family to these events. On the other hand, there also has been an alarming increase in reports of children engaging in sexually aggressive behaviors with other children and a reluctance to label these behaviors as sexual abuse. Thus, from a practical perspective, we argue that in determining whether or not sexual abuse has occurred, clinicians should focus on understanding the specific *behavior* that is reported, the context in which this behavior occurs, and the intent of the perpetrator of the behavior. The developmental level of the participants, their status relative to each other, and whether or not coercion, manipulation, or force were used are also important factors in determining that sexual behavior is abusive.

PREVALENCE

Estimates of the prevalence of sexual abuse reflect definitional problems, as well as differences in the populations sampled (i.e., clinical versus community). Estimates vary tremendously, ranging from 6 to 62% of girls and from 3 to 31% of boys (Peters, Wyatt, & Finkelhor, 1986), with higher rates found in clinical samples. Most recently, Finkelhor, Hotaling, Lewis, and Smith (1990) report on the results of a large survey (completed in 1985) that was representative of the demographics of the United States census. Using a relatively broad definition of sexual abuse (i.e., contact as well as noncontact sexual behavior), a history of sexual abuse was reported by 27% of women and 16% of men. Bagley (1990) examined prevalence rates for retrospective reports of sexual abuse by age cohorts, and found evidence that prevalence, at least among women, may be decreasing. A history of abuse was recalled by 20.8% of 18-year-olds, 33.3% of 21-year-olds, and 42.0% of 24-year-olds. He speculates that younger women increasingly have been exposed to media presentations about sexual abuse and this increased exposure may be contributing to an actual decline in instances of abuse.

Walker, Bonner, and Kaufman (1988) presented data from the American Association for Protecting Children indicating that the incidence of sexual abuse increases with the age of the child. Among children who were sexually abused, 25% were ages 0 to 5, 34.3% were ages 6 to 11, and 40.6% were ages 12 to 17. Finkelhor et al. (1990) report the average age of abuse as 9.9 years for boys and 9.6 years for girls. In his survey, about one quarter of boys and girls were abused before the age of 8 years.

Although there is agreement that sexual abuse in general tends to be underreported, many suspect that prevalence rates are underestimated for boys to a greater extent than for girls. Rates of abuse reported for clinical samples of boys are much lower than for community surveys, while the reverse is true for girls (Watkins & Bentovim, 1992). This suggests that only the most severe cases of abused boys come to the attention of the mental health community. Watkins and Bentowim (1992) give a variety of reasons for these findings including fear of homosexuality or of not being believed, differential reactions to the abuse, lack of recognition of child–child abuse, denial that abuse is committed by women, and so on. There is some consensus regarding several differences in the characteristics of sexual abuse of boys versus girls. In their review of research, Watkins and Bentovim (1992) indicate that boys are more likely than girls to experience anal penetration, to also be physically abused, to be abused by multiple perpetrators, and to be forcefully abused. There is no consensus on whether boys tend to be older or younger than girls, or whether they are more likely to be abused by strangers versus relatives.

PERPETRATORS

Who are the perpetrators of child sexual abuse? Unfortunately, this is not an easy question to answer because perpetrators are a very diverse group, including mothers, fathers, grandparents, nonrelative caregivers, family friends, strangers, and children and adolescents as well as older individuals. Perpetrators are overwhelmingly male, although it is estimated that women commit about 5% of the sexual abuse among female victims and 20% among male victims (Finkelhor, 1987). While abuse by fathers and stepfathers is most common among cases reported to child protective agencies, national community samples indicate that these individuals commit no more than 7 to 8% of all cases of sexual abuse (Finkelhor, 1987). More frequently, perpetrators include other family members (typically uncles and brothers, 16–42% of cases), and other nonrelatives (friends, neighbors, childcare workers, etc., 32–60% of cases) (Finkelhor, 1987).

Finkelhor (1984) describes the conditions that must be present for abuse to occur. First, the perpetrator must be *motivated* to relate sexually with a child. In most cases, an important emotional need is satisfied by this relationship. Many child molesters have been found to have unusual needs for power and dominance which would provide the necessary motivation to select children (who are relatively powerless) as sexual objects (Finkelhor, 1987). Moreover, the perpetrator must be sexually aroused by children and alternative, appropriate sources of sexual gratification often may be unavailable. It has been shown that perpetrators of child sexual abuse demonstrate unusual levels of sexual arousal to child stimuli such as pictures of children or children's clothing and often have difficulties with adult heterosexual relationships (Finkelhor, 1987).

Second, *internal inhibitors* must be overcome. Many factors can contribute to this including alcohol and drug use, sexualized portrayal of children in the media, stressful life events (e.g., divorce, unemployment, etc.), emotional dysfunction, and a lack of strong community sanctions (i.e., failure to prosecute or convict offenders and weak sentencing patterns). Finkelhor (1987) estimates that alcohol is involved in 19 to 70% of cases. Stermac and Segal (1989) found that child molesters differed from other groups of men (including rapists, lawyers, police, clinicians, and laypeople) in their cognitions about sexual relations with children. The men who molested children perceived more benefits to the child from the sexual contact, greater cooperation on the child's part, and less responsibility on the adult's part than did the other groups. Such cognitions could clearly contribute to the reduction of internal inhibitors. Further, in a related study, Parker and Parker (1986) found that a lack of involvement by fathers and stepfathers in the day-to-day care of infant daughters was associated with increased risk of sexual abuse. The authors speculate that this early care creates a strong emotional bond between parent and child which in turn may contribute to incest avoidance via the mechanism of inhibited sexual arousal to child stimuli.

Third, *external inhibitors* that would ordinarily prevent abuse from occurring must be overcome. The perpetrator must have access to the child and might gain this access through the physical absence of the mother through illness, death or divorce, or a mother who, for a variety of reasons (employment, emotional disturbance, etc.), is not able to protect her child. An association between maternal physical or psychological absence and an increased risk of sexual abuse among girls has been documented (Finkelhor, 1984; Russell, 1983).

Finally, the *child's resistance* also must be overcome. Factors that could contribute to this include the perpetrator's use of coercion or manipulation, the child's lack of knowledge of sexuality and abuse prevention skills, poor self-confidence, emotional distress, or physical or intellectual handicaps. Two studies (Budin & Johnson, 1989; Conte, Wolf, & Smith, 1989) have conducted interviews with convicted child molesters to determine how they engage children in sexual activities. The results indicate that perpetrators tend to prefer children who could be described as vulnerable (passive/shy, troubled, or lonely children from broken homes) and needy for attention and affection or overly friendly. Perpetrators also use a variety of methods to gain children's trust, including being a friend, playing games with the child, giving the child money or toys, or giving them special attention. Finally, various methods of threat or force are used to gain the child's compliance. These include hitting, threats to hurt loved objects, using weapons, and threats to hurt family members, plus a variety of other threats including loss of friends, loss of love, parental divorce, punishment, loss of promised rewards, and so on.

This work contributes to a better understanding of the circumstances under which sexual abuse occurs. Research on the personality dynamics of child sexual abuse perpetrators and identifying factors that predict who will become a perpetrator of sexual abuse has been less successful. Hall (1990) reviewed research on factors such as physiological measures of deviant sexual arousal, biochemical measures of testosterone, personality measures such as the Minnesota Multiphasic Personality Inventory (MMPI), and clinical variables such as a history of sexual victimization. He concluded that a history of sexual aggression was the most accurate predictor of future sexual aggression. In other words, individuals who engage in sexual aggression are most likely to continue to do so. This work strongly suggests that clinicians must be concerned about early treatment of children who engage in sexually aggressive behaviors.

Unfortunately, there are few effective treatment programs for adults who molest children. Studies of recidivism rates for child molesters indicate that reoffending is a very common problem, even for those who have received treatment, and that reconvictions often occur years after the first offense. Hanson, Steffy, and Gauthier (1993) found that over 42% of their sample of incarcerated child molesters were reconvicted of sexual or violent crimes, with 23% of these reconvicted more than 10 years after being released from prison! There was no difference in recidivism rates between those who received treatment and those who did not, even though the treated offenders all showed significant improvement on measures of personality functioning.[1] Men who engaged in incest were least likely to be reconvicted while recidivism rates for those who chose boys as victims were highest. Other factors that have been consistently associated with recidivism include never having been married and a history of sexual offenses (Hanson et al., 1993; Rice, Quinsey, & Harris, 1991). The rate of reconviction among these incarcerated child molesters is disturbingly high, yet these men make up a small percentage of those who sexually abuse children. Little or nothing is known about reoffenses among child molesters who are not convicted or who never enter the criminal justice system. It would seem likely that recidivism rates among this population would be even higher than among those who have been imprisoned.

In dealing with individual cases of child sexual abuse, the clinician may find it helpful to organize information about the alleged perpetrator according to the risk factors shown in Table 1, Chapter 4. Although psychological profiles that identify sexual abusers have no empirical validity, personality measures such as the MMPI in combination with other measures such as the Thematic Apperception Test (TAT) and Rorschach, and a clinical interview are very useful in describing general psychopathology and planning treatment.

EFFECTS OF SEXUAL ABUSE

Short-Term Effects

Despite the suggestion that children's sexual encounters with others do not necessarily lead to harmful effects, current research has clearly documented that many victims of sexual abuse evidence a variety of significant problems. In a recent review of the empirical literature, Kendall-Tackett, Williams, and Finkelhor (1993) reported that sexually abused children clearly had more symptoms than nonabused, nonclinic referred children but tended to be less symptomatic than nonabused clinic referred children. Symptoms that occurred most frequently among sexually abused children were fears, posttraumatic stress disorder (PTSD), general behavior problems, sexualized behaviors, and poor self-esteem. Of these, only PTSD and sexualized behavior occurred more

---

[1]Current treatment involving cognitive behavioral techniques and relapse prevention shows promise but there is not yet sufficient data to support its efficacy (e.g., Laws, 1989; Marshall, Laws & Barbaree, 1990).

frequently among the sexually abused children than among the nonabused clinic referred children.

Symptoms of PTSD have been found in a number of studies of the effects of abuse on children. The central features of PTSD include: (1) experiencing or witnessing an event which involves actual or threatened death or serious injury to self or others *and* responding with intense fear, helplessness, or horror; (2) reexperiencing the traumatic event (e.g., nightmares, trauma-specific reenactment in play, etc.); (3) avoiding stimuli associated with the trauma (e.g., affective numbing, or lack of general responsiveness); and (4) hyperarousal (e.g., startle responses, hypervigilance, inattentiveness, irritability or outbursts of anger, and/or difficulty sleeping) (American Psychiatric Association, 1994). McLeer and her colleagues (McLeer, Deblinger, Atkins, Foa, & Ralphe, 1988; McLeer, Deblinger, Henry, & Orvaschel, 1992) found that nearly one-half of the children in their samples of outpatient sexually abused children met the DSM-III-R criteria (American Psychiatric Association, 1987) for a diagnosis of PTSD and the majority of others exhibited one or more of the symptoms of PTSD; 80 to 86.5% had symptoms of reexperiencing, 64 to 72% showed symptoms of hyperarousal, and 48.4 to 52.4% demonstrated avoidant behaviors. Similarly, Kendall-Tackett et al. (1993) reported that symptoms of PTSD were the only symptoms found in a majority of sexually abused children across the studies in their review. Symptoms of PTSD were especially notable among preschool children, with 77% demonstrating these problems. Although many sexually abused children show symptoms of PTSD, it may be that a diagnosis of PTSD is appropriate only for the most severely abused children. McLeer et al. (1992) indicate that it is likely that the children in her study were more symptomatic than many abused children because they were referred to a tertiary care center for evaluation.

Sexualized behavior also has been found to a greater extent in sexually abused children than in nonabused nonclinical as well as nonabused clinical samples (e.g., Friedrich, Luecke, Beilke, & Place, 1992; Gale, Thompson, Moran, & Sack, 1988; Inderbitzen-Pisaruk, Shawchuck, & Hoier, 1992). This is such a consistent finding that many clinicians believe that sexualized behavior can be used as an indicator of sexual abuse. It is important to note, however, that many children who have been sexually abused do not evidence sexualized behavior, and conversely, many nonabused children do so. Thus, using sexualized behaviors as an indicator of sexual abuse can result in very high rates of false positives and false negatives.

In general, the effects of sexual abuse are extremely variable. In their review of studies, Kendall-Tackett et al. (1993) indicated that a substantial number of children had no symptoms (21 to 36%) and generally, only 20 to 30% were found to have any one symptom. They were not able to identify a set of symptoms that reliably differentiated sexually abused from nonabused children. No one symptom was found to characterize the majority of abused children and many symptoms were common to both sexually abused and nonabused clinic referred children. Thus, there is no empirical evidence for a ''sexual abuse syndrome'' and no empirically validated indicators of sexual abuse, including the presence of sexualized behavior (Berliner & Conte, 1993). Moreover, there is some question as to whether all abuse victims necessarily experience negative effects.

There is some evidence for developmentally related patterns of symptoms among sexually abused children (Kendall-Tackett et al., 1993); these are shown in Table 3.1. Because data typically have been collected cross-sectionally, it is not known whether these symptom patterns represent differential responses to sexual abuse by children at different ages, or changes in symptomatology that might be seen across time in one child as he or she matures (Kendall-Tackett et al., 1993). There is evidence that some symptoms may have a developmental course. Sexualized behavior, for example, is more prominent among preschoolers who have not yet learned societal prohibitions against sexual acting out. It is not as common among school-aged children, perhaps because they have internalized society's rules prohibiting public expression of sexuality, but it then reemerges as a problem in adolescence in the form of sexual promiscuity, prostitution, or sexual aggression.

A number of factors have been shown to mediate the effects of abuse. In two reviews (Beitchman et al., 1991; Kendall-Tackett et al., 1993), empiricial evidence was found for an increase in symptoms for children whose experience of abuse included the following: (1) a close relationship with the perpetrator; (2) high frequency and long duration of sexual encounters; (3) oral, anal, or vaginal penetration; and (4) use of force. Most important, they found that maternal support at the time of the disclosure was consistently related to children's adjustment. This should not be surprising as children who are caught in the midst of family turmoil surrounding the abuse are clearly going to suffer more than children whose families provide support for them. Moreover, for obvious reasons, these children are more likely to recant their disclosure of abuse than those who have supportive families.

In the Kendall-Tackett et al. (1993) review, the age of the child at the time of assessment was also found to be associated with an increase in symptoms, but this is confounded with the frequency and duration of abuse. Older children showed more symptoms but also were more likely to have experienced

Table 3.1   Symptoms of Sexual Abuse at Different Developmental Stages

Age	Symptoms
Preschoolers	Anxiety
	Nightmares
	General posttraumatic stress disorder
	Internalizing problems
	Externalizing problems
	Inappropriate sexual behavior
School-aged children	Fear
	Neurotic and general mental illness
	Aggression
	Nightmares
	School problems
	Hyperactivity
	Regressive behavior
Adolescents	Depression
	Withdrawal
	Suicidal or self-injurious behaviors
	Somatic complaints
	Illegal acts
	Running away
	Substance abuse

Source: Adapted from Kendall-Tackett, Williams, & Finkelhor (1993).

abuse over a longer period of time and more frequently than younger children. The impact of age at the time of the onset of abuse is not known, although one could speculate that this would interact in some way with the child's developmental stage and the particular issues that are typical of that stage (e.g., personal identity and relationships in adolescence; autonomy and control in toddlers, etc.). Further, one cannot assume that children who are sexually abused as infants will not remember the abuse and thus will not evidence any symptoms. Cases have been described in the clinical literature of children who begin to disclose abuse that occurred during infancy as they gain language and communication skills (Friedrich, 1990).

Taken together, these data on the effects of abuse provide helpful information for clinicians in assessing sexual abuse cases and planning treatment. The extent to which each factor contributes independently to the impact on the child is not known, but clearly the more factors experienced, the more likely it is that the child will have significant problems resulting from the abuse and will need extensive treatment. The clinician should be aware, however, that most studies of the effects of sexual abuse have relied on clinical populations (i.e., children referred for evaluation and/or treatment). As Finkelhor and Browne (1986) point out, "it is not clear that these findings reflect the experience of all child victims of sexual abuse . . ." (p. 69).

Long-Term Effects

Studies on the long-term effects of sexual abuse have been conducted with clinical populations, as well as through surveys of the general population. This research typically assesses clinical symptoms in adults who recall being sexually abused as children. Women who have been sexually abused as children evidence a variety of significant problems as adults (for reviews see Beitchman et al., 1992; Browne & Finkelhor, 1986; Walker et al., 1988). There is general consensus among professionals that women with a history of childhood sexual abuse experience increased rates of sexual dysfunction, homosexual experiences, anxiety and fears, depression, and suicidal ideation and behaviors. They also are at high risk for revictimization. A recent study (Springs & Friedrich, 1992) further indicates that these women may experience higher rates of health risk behaviors (e.g., smoking, excessive alcohol consumption, earlier age at first intercourse, increased numbers of sexual partners, and a lower frequency of Pap smears) and medical/gynecologic problems than women without a history of sexual abuse.

The data for male victims is less clear, largely because there tend to be fewer of them included in these studies. Males are thought to be more likely to experience gender identity confusion, and an increased likelihood of homosexual preference than are abused women (Watkins & Bentovim, 1992). Interestingly, in a study of homosexual and bisexual men by Doll et al. (1992), 37% reported a history of child sexual abuse, a percentage that is considerably higher than that for the general population of men (i.e., 16%; Finkelhor et al., 1990). Similar to women who have been sexually abused, men also have been found to have increased depression, suicidal feelings or behavior, lower self-esteem, anxiety disorders, sexual dysfunction, and relationship difficulties when compared to nonabused men (Watkins & Bentovim, 1992). There also are indications that men who are sexually abused as children are at higher risk for engaging in sexual aggression or becoming sexual abuse perpetrators, although not all perpetrators of sexual abuse have a history of sexual abuse in childhood (Watkins & Bentovim, 1992).

Factors similar to those found to mediate adjustment in the short term also have been implicated in long-term adjustment. Abuse by fathers or stepfathers, penetration, use of force, and long duration are associated with increased negative impact for both men and women (Browne & Finkelhor, 1986; Watkins & Bentovim, 1992). Despite the consistency of these findings, few studies note whether these abused men and women received treatment as children (and if so, what kind or for how long). Thus, it is not possible to determine whether these long-term negative effects are inevitable or whether they may be alleviated by prompt intervention at the time of disclosure.

Longitudinal studies are important in understanding sexual abuse because they permit examination of the course of sequelae over time and the factors that contribute to recovery. In their review, Kendall-Tackett et al. (1993) conclude that the majority of children tend to improve with time, although 6 to 19% of sexually abused children are reabused following the original disclosure. A substantial number (10 to 24%) of abused children, however, appear to get worse with time, and this raises the question of the existence of "sleeper effects." Evidence for this phenomenon lies in the fact that some children appear asymtomatic when first identified but may develop symptoms at a later time. Kendall-Tackett et al. suggest that this either could be because some children learn to suppress symptoms as a way of coping (e.g., through denial of the abuse or dissociation) or because they become traumatized only as their cognitive abilities enable them to recognize the implications of having been abused.

Just as a lack of family support contributes to the seriousness of the effects of abuse, strong support is a critical factor in the improvement of sexually abused children (Kendall-Tackett et al., 1993). There is no consistent evidence, however, that psychotherapy contributes to improvement. This lack of evidence most likely reflects vast differences in approaches to treatment, training of therapists, and quality of therapy. Finally, the impact of appearing in court has been assessed. Goodman et al. (1992) reported that children involved in legal proceedings, especially those who had to testify on several occasions, or were fearful of and had to face the perpetrator, were less well adjusted over 7 to 11 months than children who did not have to testify. Others suggest that the lengthy time delays that characterize legal proceedings may contribute to slow improvement in children who go to court (Runyon, Everson, Edelsohn, Hunter, & Coulter, 1988).

HIDDEN MEMORIES OF CHILDHOOD SEXUAL ABUSE

Although issues related to hidden (we avoid the term "repressed" because of its many controversial connotations) memories of child sexual abuse are most relevant to clinicians who work with adults, a brief discussion from the perspective of the child clinician is warranted because of the current controversy in the professional and public media (see Lindsay & Read [1994] for an excellent summary of the issues).

Most child clinicians recognize that traumatic events can affect children's behavior regardless of whether or not the child is able to verbalize his or her experience. The reason(s) this occurs is a fundamental question that is beyond the scope of this volume (see Siegel, in press), but one possible explanation is that the child does not have access to a memory of the experience. One process that might contribute to a child's inability to access a memory that is familiar to child clinicians is the use of dissociation (i.e., isolating oneself from a painful thought or experience) as a coping strategy for dealing with stress. Dissociation can interfere with memory by separating mental processes that are normally integrated (Friedrich, Jaworski, Huxsahl, & Bengtson, 1994). Traumatic experiences are thus out of the child's awareness (although the trauma can continue to influence behavior) and the child is prevented from reexperiencing the trauma through the persistence of intrusive thoughts. Dissociation is very common among children, particularly preschoolers, and is thought to be an adaptive mechanism. There is a large empirical literature demonstrating the effectiveness of teaching children dissociative strategies (e.g., distraction, relaxation, thought stopping, guided imagery, self-hypnosis, etc.) to cope with painful or traumatic medical procedures (Jay, 1988; Peterson, 1989). Thus, it makes sense that some children who are exposed to severe and chronic sexual abuse involving threats to their own or loved ones' survival, might use dissociation to cope with the abuse and that memories of the experiences would not be accessible. Lindsay and Read (1994) argue, however, that this is more likely to occur for a specific, single, highly traumatic incidence of abuse.

It follows that some adults who experience life-threatening trauma during childhood may not remember the experience(s) because they used dissociation as coping method. However, these adults may be stimulated to recall the childhood trauma by a particular experience, perhaps one related to raising their own children. On the other hand, it is important to note that adults can be induced to "recover memories" of events that did not occur (Loftus, 1993), and the risk of this happening when suggestive "memory recovery" techniques (e.g., hypnosis, guided imagery, journaling, etc.) are used is very high. Because there is no reliable method for distinguishing "true" from "false" memories, clinicians who work with clients whose symptoms suggest the possibility of child sexual abuse, are urged to decrease the risk of creating "false" memories by considering explanations other than child sexual abuse for the client's symptoms. Further, when memory recovery techniques are used, clinicians should inform their clients of the possibility of false memories and document their work through the use of video- or audiotape recordings (Lindsay & Read, 1994).

SEXUAL ABUSE IN DAY CARE SETTINGS

The use of day care has increased in the past 10 years as more mothers enter the work force. It is now rare that a child has not experienced some form of day care during the first five years of life. Not surprisingly, parents often worry that they have placed their children at increased risk of sexual abuse by leaving them in the care of others.

Finkelhor and his colleagues (Finkelhor, Williams, & Burns, 1988) addressed this concern through a survey of 270 day care settings across the United States in which sexual abuse was substantiated during the period from 1983 to 1985. They included center based day care (facilities with 6–12 children) and family day care (care provided for six or more children in the owner's home). These cases involved 1,639 victims under the age of 7 years, the majority of whom were 3 and 4 years old. From these data, Finkelhor et al. estimated the true incidence of sexual abuse cases in day care settings to be 2,500 children in 500 to 550 centers over a 3-year period. Although these are frightening statistics, Finkelhor et al. point out that when one considers the overall incidence of sexual abuse and the fact that on average many more children are cared for in day care centers than at home, in reality young children are at greater risk of sexual abuse in their own homes than in day care settings. This study did not include informal small-scale child care operations, however, and thus may underestimate the risk of sexual abuse for children in other types of day care settings.

A study by Margolin (1991) described cases of sexual abuse by nonrelated caregivers in informal arrangements or working in unlicensed, unregistered facilities. These cases represented about one-third of the substantiated sexual abuse committed by persons other than parents in Iowa during 1985 and 1986. In 31% of the sample of 325 cases, the abuse was committed by a caregiver hired by parents and used on a regular basis, often caring for the child in the parents' own home (68%). The perpetrators in these cases were more likely than expected to be female (36%) and adolescent (mean age was 16.9). Other cases involved adult friends of the child or parents (18% of cases), relatives of caregivers (16%), ad hoc caregivers (8% of cases), live-in caregivers (8%), or parents of the children's friends (6%). The majority of perpetrators (86–100%) were male.

Most disturbing about these cases is the fact that parents often were extremely careless in choosing the caregiver (e.g., had reason to believe the caregiver had a history of molesting children, left the child with someone they did not know, or left the child with someone who was intoxicated), did not attend to the child's discomfort with or dislike of a caregiver, or did not change caregiving arrangements when the child told them about being molested.

Provision of adequate day care for all families who need it is an enormous problem. Although high quality care is available, it is costly and many families are forced to rely on less than adequate arrangements. Moreover, the difficulty of finding *any* childcare, much less affordable, good quality care, is often so great that parents may be tempted to overlook signs that their child is suffering. Finkelhor et al. (1988) discuss the role that parents can play in the early detection, follow-up, and prevention of sexual abuse in day care settings. Their suggestions are summarized in Table 3.2.

Table 3.2　What Parents Can Do to Prevent Sexual Abuse in Day Care Settings

1. Visit frequently and at irregular times (e.g., pick up the child early or drop off late)
2. Insist on free access to all areas of the day care center. Locked doors and rules about when parents can visit are grounds for suspicion
3. Participate in the program as much as possible
4. Interview people who live in or visit regularly the home of the day-care provider
5. Be equally suspicious about day care in "good" and "high-risk" neighborhoods
6. Be alert to signs of distress and seek advice from the primary health care provider if any of the following problems arise:
   - Persistent reluctance to go to the center and eagerness to leave when picked up
   - Significant changes in behavior (e.g., nightmares, toileting problems, general fears, whininess) that resolve when the child is absent from day care for a period of time
   - Unusual sexual behaviors
   - Physical complaints (e.g., genital rashes, itching, bruising)
7. Discuss the possibility of sexual abuse with the child:
   - "Nothing that happens should be a secret, no matter what you are told"
   - "Tell me immediately if anyone does anything mean"
   - "Once you are home, you are safe. Day care staff have no power to harm families"
8. Teach the child about appropriate and inappropriate behaviors in the bathroom
9. Teach the child about the intimidation tactics often used to ensure children's silence:
   - "If anyone threatens you in any way, tell me right away"
   - "Mom and Dad are more important and powerful than any day care teacher. We will always protect you"

SUMMARY AND CONCLUSIONS

In summary, research in the area of child sexual abuse furthers clinicians' understanding of the issues and dynamics of this difficult problem and can inform our clinical work with these children and families. Clinicians must understand the problems inherent in defining sexual abuse. Determination of whether or not abuse has occurred is inevitably influenced by cultural and personal values regarding sexuality in general and children's sexuality in particular. The assessment and treatment process will be effective only to the extent that it reflects this understanding. Clinicians also must be aware that little is known about the personality dynamics of perpetrators and even less about effective treatment procedures for these individuals. Thus, the risks and benefits of continuing contact between the child and perpetrator must be weighed cautiously. Mental health professionals also have an important role in influencing policy decisions that arise from this research. The fact that sexual abuse is so common among childcare providers is alarming, and it is particularly disturbing that many of these investigations are so poorly handled. States and local communities must be encouraged to adopt stricter policies regarding the licensing and inspection of day care facilities and providing training for staff. Moreover, procedures for investigation of possible sexual abuse that coordinate the work of various agencies and professionals should be in place well before they are needed.

4

Assessment of Sexual Abuse

Assessment of children who are alleged to have been sexually abused is challenging, in part because there is no way to determine the truth about what happened with absolute certainty. Moreover, once an opinion about what happened is established, it is very difficult to change it. In the assessment of sexual abuse, the clinician functions as a "fact finder," gathering information and making professional judgments about the meaning of those facts. The clinician must review a number of areas to determine if there is a pattern of factors that increase or decrease the probability that abuse has occurred. It is imperative that the criteria used in making probability statements about abuse be made explicit, including the support for and limitations of each criterion (Berliner & Conte, 1993). To do this adequately, the clinician must have knowledge of child development (particularly sexual development), be familiar with recent research on memory and suggestibility, and adopt a "quasiscientific" approach which examines alternative hypotheses.

Issues of memory and suggestibility are central in the assessment of any case of child sexual abuse. Children cannot provide accurate and detailed reports about things they cannot remember. In this chapter, the research on children's memory and suggestibility is reviewed with particular focus on its clinical implications for the assessment process. This research is then integrated into a systematic approach for assessment of child sexual abuse cases.

CLINICAL IMPLICATIONS OF RESEARCH ON MEMORY AND SUGGESTIBILITY

We have found it useful to consider the variety of factors that can influence children's reports of sexual abuse in the context of an informal framework that describes the flow of information within the memory system (see Table 4.1). This framework consists of four very general themes: (1) Not everything

Table 4.1   Framework for Understanding Memory and Suggestibility

Not everything gets into memory

- Sexual abuse involves incidental as opposed to deliberate memory
- Factors that influence what is encoded incidentally include:
  Prior knowledge, especially knowledge of sexuality
  Interest value of stimuli
  Stress or trauma

What gets into memory varies in strength

- Strength of memory trace influences how easily information is recalled
- Factors that influence strength of memory trace include:
  Amount of exposure to the event
  Participation versus observation
  Age of child
  Length of interval between encoding and recall

The status of information in memory changes

- Information in memory changes during the interval between encoding and retrieval
- Factors that influence changes include:
  Prior knowledge and "scripts" for routine events
  Age
  Length of time between encoding and recall
  Repeated interviews
  Information that is misleading or inconsistent with the event
  Therapeutic procedures
- Factors that increase risk of inaccurate or false reports include:
  Misleading information given close to or during interview
  Weaker memory traces
  Misleading information given by authority figure
  Uncertainty about what happened
  Clinician or parent bias
  Books about other children who have been abused

Retrieval is not perfect

- Memory is a reconstructive versus a reproductive process
- Over time, information recalled increasingly represents what the child (or adult) believes happened versus what really happened
- Factors that influence retrieval include:
  Understanding of the purpose of the interview
  Understanding of the questions asked
  Expressive language skills
  Use of memory strategies
  Social perspective taking ability
  Temperament
  Susceptability to suggestion
  Societal view about sexuality
  Interview context
  Interviewer bias

gets into memory; (2) what gets into memory varies in strength; (3) the status of information in memory changes over time; and (4) retrieval is not perfect (Gordon, Schroeder, Ornstein, & Baker-Ward, in press; Ornstein, Larus & Clubb, 1991).

Not Everything Gets into Memory

Clinicians who interview children suspected of having been sexually abused are concerned with the retrieval of the details about the child's experience. Presumed retrieval problems, however, often are a function of the fact that some things may not be remembered because they were not entered into memory in the first place. Cases of sexual abuse involve incidental as opposed to deliberate memory at the time of encoding. That is, at the time the events are happening, the child does not know that he or she will be questioned about the experience. Several factors that influence the information that is likely to enter the child's memory system in an incidental fashion have been identified. One of these factors is the child's prior knowledge or understanding about the events in question (Chi, Glasser, & Farr, 1988; Clubb & Ornstein, 1992). Given the developmental differences in children's knowledge of sexuality (e.g., Gordon et al., 1990a) it would be expected that older children would encode more organized information about sexual matters than would younger children. It also is possible that knowledge gained through sex education or other means such as treatment may influence remembering of an earlier event that was not necessarily interpreted as "sexual" by the child at a younger age. In these cases, however, what is remembered represents a reinterpretation of the information that was originally placed in memory, and thus the details may be substantially altered.

Other factors that influence what is entered into memory include the interest value of the stimuli and stress experienced as the event is occurring. Gordon et al. (in press) reviewed the research related to these factors and concluded that children who have been sexually abused are likely to encode some central actions, even if they do not have a clear understanding of the sexual nature of those actions. They are less likely to encode details about the people involved or the location in which the events took place, despite the fact that these details are usually needed to prosecute a case. Further, there is a growing consensus that a high level of stress at the time of encoding is likely to interfere with the acquisition of information (Gordon et al., in press). Thus, events that are very traumatic are less likely to be encoded in great detail, although the child may encode a few particularly salient bits of information.

What Gets into Memory Varies in Strength

Information that is encoded and stored in the memory system can vary considerably in the strength of the memory trace, and this can, in turn, influence the ease with which that information is recalled. Stronger representations are more likely to be remembered spontaneously or in response to open-ended questions, while weaker representations may require direct or even leading questions from the interviewer for retrieval. Research on the development of memory suggests that at least three factors influence the strength of the representation in memory: (1) the *amount of exposure* to an event; (2) the *status* of the individual as a participant or observer; and (3) the *age* of the witness.

The longer and more frequently one is exposed to a stimulus event, the stronger the memory trace (Brainerd & Ornstein, 1991; Crowder, 1976). Thus, one would expect children to have a strong memory trace for repeated sexual abuse. It is important to note, however, that when children are repeatedly exposed to the same event, they form generalized representations of the event or "scripts" (Myles-Worsley, Cromer, & Dodd, 1986; Nelson, 1986). Therefore, in cases of repeated abuse, what a child recalls may represent what "usually happens" rather than the details of a specific episode. Children's scripts for repeated events also influence what is remembered as the memory trace deteriorates over time. Thus, many of the details of a specific episode of sexual abuse may be lost and what is remembered is increasingly likely to be altered to be consistent with what the child knows or believes usually happens (Myles-Worsley et al., 1986).

The strength of the memory trace is also influenced by whether the child participates in or simply observes what is happening. In cases of sexual abuse, children are more likely to be active participants rather than passive observers, and thus the resulting memory traces will be stronger than those that stem from observation (Baker-Ward, Hess, & Flanagan, 1990). With age, however, there are increases in a variety of cognitive functions that enhance the acquisition and storage of information. The result is that older children are likely to have stronger memory traces (which are more resistant to decay) than are younger children independent of whether they are participants or observers (Brainerd & Ornstein, 1991). By the time children reach the age of 9 or 10, most are able to remember the details of events about as well as adults.

This work highlights the distinction between memory as a *reconstructive* rather than a *reproductive* process. As events are repeated and as the representation weakens over time, children's memory performance increasingly reflects a reconstruction of the actual events. Moreover, the younger the child, the more susceptable he or she is to this reconstructive process because the memory traces of younger children are inherently weaker than those of older children.

The Status of Information in Memory Changes

Once information about an experience is in the memory system, its status can be changed in the interval between encoding and retrieval. Both prior knowledge of the to-be-remembered event and age influence these changes. Moreover, children who have been abused are exposed to a variety of experiences after the abuse has occurred and before they are questioned. Some of these experiences can function to improve their memory of the events in question, whereas others can alter the memory trace and/or interfere with performance. In cases of sexual abuse, experiences occurring after an event that may alter the information in the memory system include: (1) the length of the interval between the occurrence of the event and subsequent report; (2) exposure to repeated interviews; (3) provision of information that is misleading or inconsistent with the original event; and (4) participation in various therapeutic procedures (Gordon et al., in press).

Memory traces deteriorate over the time that passes between the experience of abuse and subsequent disclosure, investigative interviews, and appearance in court. Accordingly, the more closely these procedures follow the occurrence of the event, the greater the likelihood of obtaining complete and accurate accounts of the details of the experience. Unfortunately, as time passes, it is increasingly likely that the child will be exposed to repeated interviews. In some cases, repeated interviews can serve to maintain information in memory that otherwise would have been forgotten. However, repeated interviews also increase the risk that the child will be exposed to information that is misleading or inconsistent with the original experience. It has been demonstrated that individuals exposed to misleading or inconsistent postevent information are less accurate on later "tests" of memory than those who are not so exposed (e.g., Loftus, 1979). Children, particularly those under the age of 5, have been shown to be particularly susceptible to incorporating this information into their later reports (Ceci & Bruck, 1993; Ceci, Ross, & Toglia, 1987a, 1987b). Indeed, Ceci, Leichtman, and White (in press) have shown that preschool children will provide elaborate details about things that did not happen when subjected to pre- and postevent suggestive information, and that some children will hold to their misguided beliefs even in the face of mild challenges. Not all children are suggestible at all times, however. Even in the Ceci et al. (in press) study, under the most suggestive circumstances, one quarter of the 3- to 4-year-olds and two-thirds of the 5- to 6-year-olds resisted suggestion.

The important question for clinicians is not whether children are more suggestible than adults or whether younger children are more suggestible than older children, but rather under what circumstances are children more or less vulnerable to suggestion? Factors that have been shown to influence vulnerability to suggestion include the timing of the inconsistent information, the perceived prestige of the person providing the information, the relative strength of the memory trace, and the degree of certainty the child has about the material to be remembered. Thus children are more likely to be more vulnerable to suggestion when the memory trace is weaker, when the suggestion is provided by an adult as opposed to a child, when the inconsistent information is provided close to the time of the interview, and when the child is uncertain about what happened (Gordon et al., in press).

Little is known about the influence of treatment procedures on children's recollections of abuse. Ceci et al. (in press) warn that many therapeutic procedures have the potential to elicit false reports of abuse, particularly when the clinician has a strong bias about what might have happened. For instance, reading a book about a child who has been molested to a child who is only suspected of having been abused, in the context of a parent or therapist who holds a strong belief that sexual abuse must have happened, could indeed induce that child to make a false report. We were recently referred a case of a 6-year-old boy who had been interviewed by 13 individuals on 34 occasions over the previous two years! In the course of these interviews he was read at least two books about other children who had been abused. The child consistently denied that anything had happened, but his mother, acting on her belief that sexual abuse had occurred, took him to yet one more therapist, and finally, after two years, the child agreed that he had been molested. Sadly, this child probably has come to believe that sexual abuse happened when, in fact, it is very unlikely that this is the case.

Taken together, the research indicates that the process of remembering is largely one of reconstruction. Information that is stored is almost certainly altered over time. Moreover, the more time goes by, the more likely it is that memory will be reconstructed on the basis of knowledge and intervening experiences, with the resultant recall representing less and less a reproduction of what actually happened. Although repeated interviews can function to maintain memory over time, they also increase the risk that children will be exposed to misleading or inconsistent information and will incorporate this information into their reports of what happened. Finally, clinicians or parents who have strong beliefs about a child's experience can influence some children to make reports about things that did not occur.

Retrieval Is Not Perfect

Many social and cognitive factors influence the child's ability to retrieve and report stored information. The task of the interviewer is one of "cognitive diagnosis'' (Flavell, 1985; Ornstein, 1991), a process involving evaluation of the child's responses to the interview in the context of the characteristics of the child (e.g., language, temperament, memory, and intelligence), the types of questions asked, and physical and psychological environment in which the interview is conducted.

Language development is particularly important in interviewing preschool children or those with mental retardation. Children will not be able to retrieve information in response to a question if they do not understand the syntactic constructions or the particular words used by the interviewer (Saywitz, Nathanson, & Snyder, in press). Moreover, children typically try to answer questions they do not understand, resulting in confusing or misleading responses.

Children's responses to interview questions also reflect their facility with expressive language. With increases in age, there are corresponding increases in the ability to use narrative structure to organize verbal memory reports (Mandler, 1990). Consistent with this are data that indicate that preschool children require more structured questions and memory cues than do older children (e.g., Baker-Ward, Gordon, Ornstein, Larus, & Clubb, 1993). Yet increased reliance on structured questions decreases the accuracy of responses, and when the questions are of the ''yes-no'' type, accuracy of preschool children may not be above chance levels (Gordon & Follmer, 1994).

Because the limited verbal skills of preschool children often result in their not being able to report all they can remember, efforts have been made to enhance their reports through the use of dolls or other props. Unfortunately, these methods do not seem to be effective with preschool children, although they may help older children (DeLoache & Marzolf, 1993; Follmer & Gordon, 1994). It is thought that preschool children do not have the cognitive skills to understand the use of dolls or props as representations of self. (For further discussion of the use of anatomically detailed dolls in sexual abuse interviews, see the section on Guidelines for Assessment.)

Metacognitive factors such as use of memory strategies, understanding of the interview context, and the ability to take another's perspective can also influence children's ability to provide accurate and complete reports of their experiences. These factors are typically age related, so that better performance is expected of school-aged children than preschoolers. Moreover, the relative lack of metacognitive skills may contribute to confusing, inconsistent, and even inaccurate reports from very young children. For instance, because a preschool child typically cannot take another's perspective, he or she may make the assumption that the interviewer already knows the answers to the questions and may fail to provide sufficient information for the interviewer to make sense out of the response (Saywitz et al., in press). This may be particularly true in the case of repeated interviews. Further, the child may change his or her answers when the same questions are asked repeatedly, particularly within the same interview, because of the belief that the first answer must have been incorrect or else the question would not be repeated (Ornstein et al., 1991; Siegal, Waters, & Dinwiddy, 1988).

Personality and emotional factors may also affect recall performance. Temperamental characteristics such as a child's ease in new situations and tendency to approach others have been shown to be positively associated with the ability to provide details of an experience (Gordon et al., 1993; Merritt, Spiker, & Ornstein, 1993). Further, there is some evidence indicating that suggestibility may be considered a personality "trait" that is related to recall performance (Clarke-Stewart, Thompson, & Lepore, 1989). Thus, leading questions or postevent misleading information may affect some children more than others.

The prevailing social views about sexuality also may influence children's reports of abuse. When children become aware of societal attitudes, nudity and sexuality may be associated with embarrassment and secrecy, if not punishment, in their minds and they may be reluctant to discuss sexual matters. Saywitz, Goodman, Nicholas, and Moan (1991) found that 7-year-olds were less willing to verbally report genital touch than were 5-year-olds but that doll-aided direct questions increased disclosure for these older children.

Recall is also influenced by the context in which the interview takes place. A skilled interviewer can enhance recall by providing age appropriate toys and furniture, by orienting the child to the purpose of the interview, and by helping the child feel comfortable. These arrangements help to reduce the child's distress, and in turn, lower stress results in better performance. The interview context also includes the interviewer's preexisting ideas about what did or did not happen and these ideas can significantly influence the information recalled. Pettit, Fegan, and Howie (1990) found that interviewers who were misled about children's experience prior to an interview elicited more inaccurate information from children than those who were not misled. Moreover, the inaccurate information was consistent with the interviewer's belief about what the child had experienced. Thus, it appears that interviewers who strongly believe that sexual abuse has occurred, could influence a child to make a false accusation.

It seems obvious that interviewers should be trained to conduct neutral interviews, avoiding leading and suggestive questions. Unfortunately, results of a study by Pettit et al. (1990) suggest that such training may not always be effective. They trained interviewers to ask only neutral questions but found that at later child interviews, about one-third of the questions were leading despite this training.

Taken together, the research reviewed on the memory process provides important information for clinicians who work with children who may have been sexually abused. The validity of the child's report is ultimately dependent on the extent to which the interviewer can gather and integrate information from many sources, including the child, in an unbiased and objective manner. The results of this process are critical in not only protecting the child from a harmful situation but also protecting adults from false accusations. There is no right way to interview all children but current research provides some guidelines for the assessment process.

GUIDELINES FOR ASSESSMENT

A number of guidelines for evaluation of suspected sexual abuse in children and adolescents recently have been proposed (American Academy of Child and Adolescent Psychiatry, 1988; American Professional Society on the Abuse of Children, 1990; Lamb, 1994). The essential features of these documents are summarized in this section with the addition of more specific information on assessment methods (e.g., using questionnaires, assessing development, etc.) and interpreting the assessment data.

Referral for assessment of sexual abuse can potentially involve four different types of cases. Each of these types of cases involve different issues, and therefore different assessment and treatment processes. The four types are: (1) The clinician is asked to determine whether or not sexual abuse has occurred. In these cases, the assessment must include a structured protocol that takes into account recent empirical work on children's memory and suggestibility as well as the potential involvement of the child in the legal system. (2) The clinician is asked to determine whether or not sexual abuse has occurred, *but* the child has been interviewed regarding the alleged abuse on one or more previous occasions. This assessment must include careful review of all relevant background information including the records (ideally verbatim transcripts) of all previous interviews. This information should be interpreted in light of current research on children's memory and suggestibility and risk factors for sexual abuse (see Table 4.2). It may neither be preferable nor necessary to reinterview the child (American Professional Society on the Abuse of Children, 1990). Rather, the clinician's opinion about the alleged abuse may be based on this review of existing records. (3) Sexual abuse has been substantiated and the clinician is asked to plan a treatment program. In these cases, the focus of the assessment is on acknowledging the abuse and determining the treatment needs of the child and family. (4) The clinician is asked to plan a treatment program for a child when abuse has not been substantiated, yet the parent has continuing concern regarding the child's behavior(s) and may even express a belief that abuse may have occurred. The focus of assessment in this instance should be on the behaviors of concern *without* making the assumption that abuse has occurred. It is imperative in these cases that the clinician maintain a neutral attitude toward the possibility of abuse.

The guidelines for assessment presented in this section are based on the memory research outlined above and also on clinical experience. A brief summary of the essential features of the guidelines are presented in Table 4.2. The guidelines are organized in a stepwise fashion to assist clinicans in this difficult but important work.

The Referral

Clarifying the Referral Question

Sexual abuse cases can be referred by a variety of people including parents, protective services workers, police, physicians, attorneys, and others. In assessing these cases, it is most important to clarify the referral question(s) so that the clinician and the referring person are in agreement about the focus of the assessment. The clinician must then decide which questions can reasonably be answered according to the facts of each case and to carefully focus the assessment on only those questions.

When assessment is requested to determine if sexual abuse has occurred, we have found that the questions usually center around four issues, although not all cases involve all issues. These are: (1) verifying the alleged abuse; (2) determining the emotional/behavioral functioning of the child and the need for treatment; (3) determining the functioning of other family members, including their ability to provide protection for the child; and (4) making recommendations about child custody, placement, and treatment. If abuse has already been substantiated, the clinician is obviously not being asked to verify the abuse and should move directly to assessing the needs of the child and family.

Setting the Stage

Gathering Background Information

Before interviewing the child and/or family, the clinician should contact all persons who are involved in the case to determine their roles, to find out what

Table 4.2   Steps for Assessment of Child Sexual Abuse

The referral

Clarify the referral question and type of case
    Initial investigation of sexual abuse
    Second or third (or more) opinion
    Plan treatment for substantiated abuse case
    Plan treatment for unsubstantiated abuse case

Setting the stage

Gather background information
    Contact all involved people
    Number and type of previous interviews
    Transcripts of previous interviews
    Nature of initial disclosure, if any
    Child's behavioral changes
    Results of medical examination
    Brief family history: marital status, living arrangements, custody, etc.
    Brief developmental history
    Risk factors
Use questionnaires
    Child Behavior Checklist
    Child Sexual Behavior Inventory
    Parenting Stress Index
Arrange for audio- or videotaping
Arrange a "child friendly" setting

Parent interview

Determine if child will or will not be present
Query specific areas
    Sex education done, if any
    Parenting models
    Attitudes and values about parenting
    Child management strategies
    Child's day-to-day routines and functioning
    Changes in child's behavior
    Parent sexual history
    Parent and family perceptions of current situation
    Nature of child's initial disclosure, if any
Determine need for parent psychological evaluation

Child interview

Establish rapport
    Explain purpose of interview
    Explain what will happen during session(s)

(Continued)

Table 4.2   (Continued)

Child interview

Age appropriate play activities
   General questions about child's interests and activities
Assess development
   Language comprehension and expression
   Intellectual functioning
   Memory skills
   Emotional status
   Knowledge of sexuality
   Suggestibility
   Perceptions of family members
   Emotional problems and coping skills
Ask about sexual abuse
   Explain interviewer's lack of knowledge about what happened
   Explain need to tell only about things that really happened
   Begin with open-ended questions
   Ask directly about abuse if child does not volunteer this
   Do not use books about other children who have been abused
   Do not pressure child to disclose if none is forthcoming
Use of anatomically detailed dolls
   Useful for older children who are nonverbal or embarrassed
   May not be helpful for preschool children
   May elicit false reports
   Do not use as a "test" of sexual abuse

Evaluate the assessment data

Review the video- audiotape
   Assess responses relative to "stimulus" that elicited them
   Assess responses relative to criteria for credibility
      Details about context of abuse
      Details about sexual activity
      Description of emotional state during abuse
Review data in context of multiple factors
   Nature and context of sexual behavior:
      Description of the behavior in question
      Conditions under which behavior occurred
      How long ago did the reported event(s) occur?
   Motivation or intent of sexual behavior:
      Was the behavior motivated by sexual gratification?
   Characteristics of initial disclosure:
      Under what conditions was the disclosure made?
      What motivated reporting?
      What was response of parent(s) especially mother?

Table 4.2   (Continued)

Evaluate the assessment data

Characteristics of child:
  Age and developmental level (language and cognitive skills, sexual knowledge)
  Current and prior emotional status
  Behavior changes or symptoms
  Excessive stressors or environmental instability
Characteristics of alleged perpetrator:
  Significant psychopathology
  Alcohol or drug use at time of alleged abuse
  Stress and coping skills
  Previous history of sexual abuse
  History of antisocial behavior or criminal record
  Availability of appropriate sexual outlet
Characteristics of family:
  Social isolation
  History of inadequate parenting
  Marital status, especially divorce or custody conflict
  Substance abuse
  Stress/instability
Social/cultural context:
  Use of day care
  Sexual attitudes
Consider alternative hypotheses to explain data

information has already been gathered, and to promote collaboration. This step is particularly important if the case is likely to be prosecuted, if the clinician is being asked for a second opinion, or if the clinician is asked to plan treatment and abuse has not been substantiated. In reviewing background information, however, the clinician must be neutral as to whether abuse actually occurred or not.

The background information to be gathered at this stage in the assessment process includes the number, type, and, if possible, transcripts of prior interviews, the nature of the child's initial disclosure (or, if there is no disclosure, the reason why abuse is suspected), behavioral changes evidenced by the child, results of a medical examination, and a brief family and developmental history. Walker, Bonner, and Kaufman (1988) suggest that risk assessment is helpful in organizing background data. Table 4.3 presents many of the factors associated with poor outcome in families where sexual abuse has occurred. Information about each of these factors should be gathered during the assess-

Table 4.3   Risk Factors Associated with Poor Outcome in Sexually Abusive Families

Child risk factors
    Poor relationship with nonabusing parent
    Preexisting behavioral or emotional problems
    Intellectual or physical handicaps
    Use of threats or force, or injury to the child
    Abuse over a long time or many incidents
    Age 13 years or older
    Family relationship to perpetrator
    Few or no friends or age appropriate activities
    Court appearance without adequate preparation
    Long delays in legal proceedings
Nonabusing parent risk factors
    Failure to believe child
    Blaming others or child for abuse
    Excessive dependence on abusing spouse
    Inability or unwillingness to protect child
    Resistance to help, distrust
    History of inadequate parenting
    Social isolation
    Alcohol or drug abuse
    Significant psychopathology
    Intellectual handicaps
Perpetrator risk factors
    Denial of abuse
    Blaming others or child for abuse
    Lack of remorse, concerns only for self
    History of sexual abuse of self or others
    History of antisocial behavior or criminal record
    Significant psychopathology
    Alcohol or drug abuse
    Significant life stress and poor coping skills
    No normal sexual outlet
    History of inappropriate parenting
Social and environmental risk factors
    Isolated family
    Marital conflict or distress
    Single-parent family
    Stepparent family
    Overly restrictive or permissive sexual attitudes
    Low socioeconomic status
    Environmental instability
    Environmental stress (e.g., unemployment)

ment, and used to address questions such as whether there is a need for treatment or whether the child can safely be returned home. The presence of any one or two factors may not necessarily be of concern. Rather, the accumulation and interaction of risk factors determine outcome in most cases.

Often one or both parents are not available during an investigation, either because the child has been removed from the home or a parent is suspected of perpetrating the abuse. In these cases, information about the child's current living circumstances should be obtained and a plan should be made to gather information about the parents and family.

Questionnaires

Depending on the specific questions to be addressed and the availability of parents to complete them, questionnaires and checklists are helpful in completing the task of gathering background information. A basic demographic questionnaire can inform the clinician about the family circumstances; an example is shown in Figure 1. The Child Behavior Checklist (Achenbach & Edelbrock, 1983) has been used extensively in research with child sexual abuse victims and provides information on sexual behavior, PTSD, and other emotional or behavioral problems that can corroborate sexual abuse (e.g., Friedrich, Belke & Urquiza, 1988).

Another measure of sexual behavior, the Child Sexual Behavior Inventory-Revised (CSBI-R) (Friedrich, 1990; Friedrich et al., 1992), consists of questions about specific types and frequencies of sexual behavior exhibited by children. This instrument has been standardized and validated by comparing responses of parents of sexually abused children (ages 3–12) with those of parents of nonabused children of the same ages. The CSBI-R, along with the means and standard deviations for the normal and abused samples, is shown in Table 4.4. In using data from these questionnaires, especially the CSBI-R, the clinician must understand that there are *no* empirically validated behavioral indicators of sexual abuse, including sexualized behavior (Berliner & Conte, 1993). Thus, it is critical that information about sexual behavior be evaluated in light of children's normative sexual behavior and knowledge. It is not unusual for children to be referred for sexual abuse evaluation because they are engaging in sexual behavior or express knowledge that is typical for their developmental stage but not recognized as such by the adults around them. For instance, two brothers, ages 3 and 5 years, were referred for assessment of suspected abuse because their grandmother caught them behind the sofa touching each other's penises. Among children at these ages, this behavior is typical and would not necessarily indicate sexual abuse.

PARENT QUESTIONNAIRE

DATE_____   FORM COMPLETED BY_____

CHILD'S NAME_____ M_____ F_____ BIRTHDATE_____

ADDRESS_____
      Street   City   State   County   Zip Code

HOME PHONE_____BUSINESS PHONE (mother)_____(father)_____

WHO REFERRED THE CHILD?_____
                name   address

CHILD'S PRIMARY PHYSICIAN_____ INSURANCE COMPANY_____

FAMILY

Father's Name_____Birthdate_____

Occupation_____ Educational Level_____ No. of Dependents _____

Mother's Name_____Birthdate_____

Occupation_____ Educational Level_____ No. of Dependents_____

Date of Marriage _____Present Marital Status_____

With whom does the child live: Birth Parents?_____ Adoptive Parents? _____

       Foster Parents: _____ Other (Specify) _____

List all other persons living in the home.

Name   Age   Relationship to child   Present Health

_____   _____   _____   _____

_____   _____   _____   _____

_____   _____   _____   _____

_____   _____   _____   _____

_____   _____   _____   _____

_____   _____   _____   _____

List any other people who care for the child a significant amount of time.

Name   Relationship to child (grandmother, neighbor, etc.)

_____   _____

_____   _____

_____   _____

_____   _____

CHILD

Pregnancy and Birth: any complications? _____yes _____no

If yes, briefly explain: _____

Figure 1. Parent Questionnaire

Developmental Milestones: (Ages) Sitting _____ Walking _____ Talking _____ Toilet Trained _____

Medical Problems? _____ yes _____ no

If yes, briefly explain: _____

_____

What are your child's favorite recreational or extracurricular activities: _____

_____

_____

Who generally disciplines the child? _____

What methods are used?_____

_____

_____

Do parents agree on methods of discipline? _____ yes _____ no

Elaborate, if no: _____

_____

_____

Compared to other children his/her age, how well does your child:

	Worse	About the Same	Better
1. Get along with his/her brothers and sisters?	_____	_____	_____
2. Get along with other children?	_____	_____	_____
3. Behave with his/her parents?	_____	_____	_____
4. Plan and work by himself/herself?	_____	_____	_____

SCHOOL HISTORY

Has child been enrolled in nursery or day care? _____ yes _____ no   If yes, at what age? _____

Has child attended kindergarten? _____ yes _____ no   If yes, at what age? _____

Has child begun elementary school? _____ yes _____ no   At what age did he/she enter 1st grade? _____

What is child's present grade? _____

If your child has ever been to school (including nursery, kindergarten and grade school) complete the following for all classes beginning with nursery and ending with current placement. Please indicate if your child repeated or is in a special class (gifted, learning disabled, emotionally handicapped, etc.)

Grade	School	Comments
_____	_____	_____
_____	_____	_____
_____	_____	_____
_____	_____	_____
_____	_____	_____

Figure 1. (Continued)

Current school performance - for children aged 6 and older:

_____ Does not go to school

	Failing	Below Average	Average	Above Average
a. Reading	_____	_____	_____	_____
b. Writing	_____	_____	_____	_____
c. Arithmetic or math	_____	_____	_____	_____
d. Spelling	_____	_____	_____	_____

Other academic subjects (history, science, foreigh language, geography, etc.)

e. _____	_____	_____	_____	_____
f. _____	_____	_____	_____	_____
g. _____	_____	_____	_____	_____
h. _____	_____	_____	_____	_____

PARENTAL CONCERNS

What do you feel is your child's main problem? _____

_____

_____

What do you feel caused your child's problem? _____

_____

_____

What have you been told by doctors, teachers and/or others about your child's problems? _____

_____

_____

Has this child had any other mental health evaluations or treatment? _____ yes _____ no

If yes, please explain _____

_____

Has any other member of the child's immediate family had mental health treatment? _____ yes _____ no

If yes, please explain _____

_____

Other comments: _____

_____

May we contact the child's primary physician? _____ to receive information

                                               _____ to give information

_____
(Signed) Parent or Guardian

Figure 1. (Continued)

Table 4.4   Child Sexual Behavior Inventory-Revised (CSBI-R)

Please circle the number that tells how often your child has shown the following behaviors recently or in the last 6 months.

	Never = 0		1–3 times a month = 2
	Less than 1 time a month = 1		At least 1 time a month = 3

1.	0	1	2	3	Dresses like the opposite sex
2.	0	1	2	3	Talks about wanting to be the opposite sex
3.	0	1	2	3	Touches sex (private) parts in public places
4.	0	1	2	3	Masturbates with hand
5.	0	1	2	3	Scratches anal or crotch area or both
6.	0	1	2	3	Touches or tries to touch mother's or other women's breast
7.	0	1	2	3	Masturbates with object
8.	0	1	2	3	Touches other people's sex (private) parts
9.	0	1	2	3	Imitates the act of sexual intercourse
10.	0	1	2	3	Puts mouth on another child's or adult's sex parts
11.	0	1	2	3	Touches sex (private) parts when at home
12.	0	1	2	3	Uses words that describe sex acts
13.	0	1	2	3	Pretends to be opposite sex when playing
14.	0	1	2	3	Makes sexual sounds (sighing, moaning, heavy breathing, etc.)
15.	0	1	2	3	Asks others to engage in sexual acts with him or her
16.	0	1	2	3	Rubs body against people or furniture
17.	0	1	2	3	Inserts or tries to insert objects in vagina or anus
18.	0	1	2	3	Tries to look at people when they are nude or undressing
19.	0	1	2	3	Imitates sexual behavior with dolls or stuffed animals
20.	0	1	2	3	Shows sex (private) parts to adults
21.	0	1	2	3	Tries to view picture of nude or partially dressed people
22.	0	1	2	3	Talks about sexual acts
23.	0	1	2	3	Kisses adults not in the family
24.	0	1	2	3	Undresses in front of others
25.	0	1	2	3	Sits with crotch or underwear exposed
26.	0	1	2	3	Kisses other children not in the family
27.	0	1	2	3	Talks in a flirtatious manner
28.	0	1	2	3	Tries to undress other children or adults against their will (opening pants, shirts, etc.)

(Continued)

Table 4.4   (Continued)

29.	0	1	2	3	Asks to view nude or sexually watch explicit TV shows (may include video movies or HBO-type shows)
30.	0	1	2	3	When kissing, tries to put tongue in other person's mouth
31.	0	1	2	3	Hugs adults he or she does not know well
32.	0	1	2	3	Shows sex (private) parts to children
33.	0	1	2	3	If a girl, overly aggressive: if a boy, overly passive
34.	0	1	2	3	Seems very interested in the opposite sex
35.	0	1	2	3	If a boy, plays with girls' toys: if a girl, plays with boys' toys

36. Other sexual behaviors (please describe) _____

Total scores for normative and abused groups for the CSBI-R

Subjects	Age (years)	Normative		Abused	
		M	SD	M	SD
Boys	2–6	10.60	7.64	20.51	18.18
Girls		11.72	8.32	21.19	18.07
Boys	7–12	5.56	5.95	16.69	15.37
Girls		5.35	6.14	11.19	12.92

Source: Friedrich et al. (1992).

Finally, the Parenting Stress Index (Abidin, 1990) provides preliminary information about the child's temperamental characteristics and sources of stress for the child's parent(s) apart from the abuse.

Taping the Interview

If the assessment is for purposes of determining whether or not abuse has occurred, arrangements should be made to audio- or videotape the child's interview prior to seeing the child and/or parents. Although some argue against taping the interview, we think this record serves two very important purposes. First, it can help to minimize the number of interviews to which the child is exposed. Second, after the interview is completed, the clinician can review the questions asked and the manner in which they were asked, and evaluate the child's reponses to these questions.

Arranging the Setting

The setting in which the child will be interviewed for alleged sexual abuse should be arranged to facilitate the child's recall. A "child friendly" environment with age appropriate toys and props such as crayons and paper, a doll house and dolls should be provided. The interview should be conducted as soon after the referral as possible, within a few days to a week at most. A speedy interview is particularly important for preschool children.

Parent Interview

The nature of the parent interview will vary depending on the purpose of the assessment. When the purpose is to plan a treatment program, it is important that a judgment that abuse occurred is made prior to the parent interview. This is critical because our approach to treatment is to interview the parent with the child present. In order to decrease the pressure on the child, we ask the parent (or other adult) to tell us the details of the abuse, including how it was first disclosed, while checking periodically with the child to verify the information. This informs the child that it is all right to talk about sexual matters and that there will be no secrets. Reactions of the parent(s) and other family members to the abuse should be noted as an indication of their ability to provide support for the child. The parent(s) should also be asked about any sex education the child has received and what terms for sexual body parts are used by the family.

If the referral question concerns the ability of a parent to care for and protect the child, a separate parent interview is likely to be necessary. The parent's "parenting models," attitudes and values about parenting, and disciplinary practices should be assessed. Information about the child's day-to-day functioning at home and school should also be gathered at this time, with an emphasis on changes in the child's behavior since the abuse occurred. It is often relevant to briefly assess a parent's sexual history and sexual attitudes and values, although this is best done in the absence of the child. Questions should be asked about the parent's sex education and age at first sexual experience; it should also be determined whether the parent was ever molested as a child.

When the referral is for treatment of a child who is suspected or believed (by parents or others) to have been abused but the abuse has not been substantiated, the child should not be included in any discussion of sexual abuse and the child should not be questioned regarding suspected abuse. Rather, the focus should be on the behaviors of concern and the clinician should entertain hypotheses other than sexual abuse to explain these behaviors. In the course of treatment, the child might disclose information about abuse; for example, when the clinician gives the child information about sexuality. The clinician must then evaluate the child's "disclosure" in the context of the child's history and the events that precipitated the disclosure.

If the assessment is being conducted for purposes of investigation of sexual abuse, the initial parent interview is usually brief and the child is not present. The focus of this interview should be on the parent's perceptions of the situation, the family's reactions, and the way in which the abuse was initially disclosed. Details of the child's initial disclosure are important because this is often the most accurate account of the abuse; disclosure is often precipitated by an event associated with the circumstances of the abuse (bathing, watching TV, going to bed, etc.). The clinician should determine where and how the disclosure occurred, what the exact words used by the child were, and what was said or done in response. In cases in which the child has not verbally reported sexual abuse, detailed information should be gathered about the behaviors or events that lead to the suspicion of abuse. In a recent case assessed in our clinic, for example, the mother had been worried about "autisticlike" behavior exhibited by her $2^{1}/_{2}$-year-old daughter when she returned from visits with her father for at least one year prior to the referral. It was only when her daughter complained of a "sore bottom" that the mother began to suspect sexual abuse. A subsequent medical examination revealed physical evidence of vaginal penetration but the child never verbally disclosed the abuse, even when asked directly.

In cases in which the suspected abuser is a parent, it is often useful to request (or conduct) a psychological evaluation of both parents. Although there is no psychological profile that can identify sexual abusers, the data from this evaluation can often corroborate the clinician's hypothesis about what might have happened. Certainly, evidence of significant psychopathology, or any of the other risk factors presented in Table 3, in one or both parents, would raise suspicions about the possibility of abuse, whereas the absence of such findings may support an alternative hypothesis. For instance, we have seen cases (typically involving issues of parental divorce and child custody) in which the mother alleges that the father has molested the child, but the mother evidences significant psychopathology, whereas the father does not.

Establishing Rapport

Regardless of the referral question, the clinician must have rapport with a child before discussion of sensitive issues will be productive. It is important that the child be informed about the reason for the interview, what will happen during the session(s), and what is expected of the child. If the purpose of assessment is investigation of abuse, the interviewer might ask the child:

"Do you know why you are here today?" and, if no response is forthcoming (which is usually the case), continue with "You are here because ——— is worried that something bad (uncomfortable, yucky, etc.) might have happened to you. I talk with lots of children who have had bad things happen to them, so it's okay for you to tell me anything you want to, but you should only tell me about things that really happened. First, I think we should get to know each other better. We can color for a while if you'd like to. Then I'll ask you some questions. Does that sound okay?"

Some general conversation about the child's interests and accomplishments is appropriate prior to asking about the abuse (for other examples of preparation instructions, see Saywitz, Geiselman, & Bornstein, 1992).

If the purpose of the assessment is to plan treatment for a child for whom abuse has been substantiated, the child is already aware of the purpose of the session since he or she was present in the parent interview. The child simply needs to be told how the session will be conducted and what is expected of him or her. If the assessment is to plan treatment for a child for whom the abuse has *not* been substantiated, the child can be told:

Your parent (teacher, doctor) is concerned that you have been having trouble with sleeping (masturbating in public, not wanting to visit daddy, curiousity about other kids' sexual parts, or whatever the behavior that is of concern). I talk with lots of children who are having the same problem(s). Together we will try to understand what is troubling you and what we can do to make things better for you. Today I would like to get to know you better and ask you some questions about your school, friends and family.

Assessing Development

Regardless of the referral question, the child's developmental status should be assessed, formally if there appears to be some concern in this area (e.g., the child has documented learning or language problems) and informally if the child appears to be developing normally. Areas to assess include language comprehension and expression, intellectual level, memory skills, emotional status, and knowledge of sexuality.

In cases involving investigation of sexual abuse, this assessment provides a framework for deciding how questions will be asked, what props will be used, and how the child's responses will be evaluated. Yuille, Hunter, Joffe, and Saparniuk (1993) suggest that the child be asked to describe two specific past experiences (e.g., a birthday or last Christmas) the details of which can be verified by parents. This allows the interviewer to model the form of the interview (e.g., asking lots of questions) and the child to practice giving complete descriptions; however, the clinician should be aware that under the age of 5 years, free recall of details is more difficult than for older children. Specific questions such as, "Tell me one thing you got for your last birthday" are easier for younger children to answer than open-ended questions such as "Tell me about your last birthday." The child's susceptibility to suggestion can be assessed by challenging some of his or her responses to questions about the details of such events (Wehrspann, Steinhauer, Klajner-Diamond (1987). The clinician could say, for example, "You didn't really get a bicycle for your birthday, did you?" or "Your mom said you got a doll" when the child did not receive a doll.

The language used in the interview must be consistent with the child's language comprehension level. This is particularly important for preschool children who have trouble with vocabulary, multiple syllable words, and syntax. Check out what the child actually understands, since children often think that they know the meaning of a word or a question when in fact they do not, or only have a partial understanding. To assess the child's understanding, request definitions or explanations, rather than accepting "yes" reponses to "Do you understand?" When changing the topic, make sure the child is aware of the transition. (For suggestions on conducting a "cognitive interview", see Geiselman, Saywitz, & Bornstein, 1993).

Regardless of the referral question, children's knowledge of sexuality is an important area of development to assess. We assess knowledge in the following areas: body parts and functions (including sexual and nonsexual body parts); gender differences and gender identity; pregnancy and birth;

sexual behavior (masturbation and sexual intercourse); and abuse prevention (e.g., "What are the private parts?" "What should you do if someone tries to touch your private parts?"). Young children respond better to concrete stimuli, so we use pictures of nude boys and girls and men and women as we ask questions in these areas. Anatomically detailed dolls also could be used for this purpose. Assessment of sexual knowledge often elicits emotional reactions from a child who has been sexually abused, and sometimes spontaneously precipitates discussion of the child's sexual experience.

Assessment of current emotional status as well as that prior to the suspected abuse is important. The existence of recent emotional problems such as unusual fears, anxiety, guilt, and poor self-esteem can provide corroborative evidence regarding the child's report of abuse or the parent's suspicion of abuse. The Pictorial Scale of Perceived Competence and Social Acceptance for Young Children (Harter & Pike, 1984) and the Self-Perception Profile for Children (Harter, 1983) are useful for assessing self-esteem. Maladaptive responses and poor coping skills can be assessed in children ages 6 to 15 with the Roberts Apperception Test for Children (McArthur & Roberts, 1982). Additional information can be obtained by observing the child's play and noting unusual themes (aggression, fear, guilt, etc.), over- or underactivity, and intense or unusual reactions to ordinary stimuli.

The clinician can assess the child's general perceptions of members of the family through a variety of methods and this information can be particularly informative if a family member is suspected of the abuse. With preschool children, family drawings or dollhouse play can be used as stimuli for discussion about what the child likes and dislikes about each person and what kinds of things they do together. Extreme or intense reactions (fear, anger, hostility, etc.) to a specific family member(s) is especially important to note. For instance, in a case we recently assessed, a 4-year-old girl was so afraid of her grandfather (who allegedly had molested her) that she could not draw a picture of him and refused to talk about him. At the same time, she was very open and expressed positive feelings about other family members.

Questioning about Sexual Abuse

When the interview involves questions specific to sexual abuse, the clinician should begin with a brief statement that he or she does not know what happened, so it is important for the child to provide as much detail as possible. The interview should begin with open-ended questions (e.g., "Tell me about your stepfather." "What do you like/dislike about him?"). This is important because the types of questions asked are directly related to the accuracy and completeness of the child's recall, as well as the interviewer's (and others') perceptions of the credibility of the child's report. Preschool children will require more direct and specific questions but their responses to these questions may be difficult to interpret. In particular, "yes–no" questions are problematic for preschoolers and the validity of their responses must be viewed cautiously.

At some point, if the child has not volunteered information, he or she must be asked directly about the possibility of sexual abuse. The question, "Has anyone ever touched your (use the child's own label for genitalia)" is very ambiguous because children's bottoms are often touched for a variety of nonabusive reasons. "Yes" responses require further clarification (e.g., "What did Dad do when he touched your bottom?") and if none is forthcoming, these responses must be interpreted cautiously. In a case recently referred to us, a 3-year-old boy (with a history of encopresis which had been treated with enemas and suppositories) had complained to his mother of a sore bottom. She asked him if anyone had ever "touched his bottom" and he responded "Daddy poked my bottom." The mother (who was recently separated from the father) interpreted this as possible sexual abuse, yet later, when asked to elaborate, the boy would only indicate that his father had poked the side of his hip.

It is not uncommon for clinicians or parents to attempt to elicit a disclosure by reading the child a book about another child who has been abused. This is not appropriate because it introduces information that can influence the child's report. For example, in several cases referred to us (including the case of the 3-year-old described above), the book *I Can't Talk About It* by Doris Sanford (1986) was read to the children during the assessment process. This particular book (and we are sure others as well) presents detailed descriptions of a father who molested a child and we think has potential to elicit a false accusation. More general books on sex education or sex abuse prevention, such as the series by Sol Gordon (Gordon, 1983; Gordon & Gordon, 1974; Gordon & Gordon, 1984) can be used during assessment or treatment in most all cases.

Using Anatomically Detailed Dolls

The use of anatomically detailed (AD) dolls is very controversial (Everson & Boat, 1994) and there are data indicating that use of dolls in sexual abuse interviews may not facilitate preschool children's reports of sexual abuse

(DeLoache & Marsolf, 1993; Gordon et al., 1993). Concerns regarding the use of AD dolls center around two important issues: (1) Do the dolls elicit false reports of sexual abuse? (2) How are the dolls most appropriately used to assess sexual abuse?

In a recent review of the research on AD dolls, the Anatomical Doll Task Force (American Psychological Association, 1994) concluded that clinicians should not be discouraged from using AD dolls in interviews with sexually abused children. However, they must be particularly cautious in the use of these dolls with preschool children because the tendency for these younger children to be more suggestible may lead them to make false reports of sexual abuse when interviewed with AD dolls (see a study by Bruck, Ceci, Francoeur, and Renick described in the Report of the Anatomical Doll Task Force, American Psychological Association, 1994). Further, although sexualized play with the dolls is uncommon among nonabused children, it does happen; some children may exhibit such play even though they have not been abused (Boat & Everson, 1994; Everson & Boat, 1990). Anatomically detailed dolls are clearly not appropriately used as a diagnostic "test" of sexual abuse; their use is not standardized and they have no demonstrated reliability or validity. Further, there is no evidence that the information gained with AD dolls is enhanced or diminished by the use of a structured protocol. In sum, therefore, it seems most reasonable to consider AD dolls as one of many possible aids in conducting clinical interviews with children who are suspected of being sexually abused. In this regard, they may facilitate communication with children who have limited vocabulary with which to talk about sexual matters, or are too embarrassed to describe the sexual details of an abuse experience.

EVALUATING THE ASSESSMENT DATA

The first step in evaluating the assessment data for investigation of abuse is to review the audio- or videotape of the child's interview and assess each critical response in light of the stimulus that was required to elicit it. Was the response relatively spontaneous or heavily cued (e.g., "Tell me about Uncle Joe" versus "Did Daddy touch your bottom?"). A judgment about the overall credibility of the child's report can then be made. Faller (1988) suggests three criteria for evaluating credibility, which she validated by examining the reports of 103 children in cases where the perpetrators had admitted all or some aspects of the abuse. These criteria include: (1) *information about the context* of the abuse, including where and when it occurred, what clothing was worn and what was removed during the abuse, where other family members were when it occurred, what the perpetrator said, and any unusual events that occurred (e.g., "I always wore my pajamas backwards to make it harder for him"); (2) *a detailed description* of the sexual activity; and (3) *the child's emotional state* at the time of the abuse and/or during the telling.

Evaluation of these aspects of a child's report must be made with the child's developmental status in mind, because younger children have more difficulty meeting these criteria than do older children despite the fact that their reports may be as accurate (Gordon & Follmer, 1994). deYoung (1987) specifies some of the areas that are likely to be problematic for preschool children: (1) Descriptions may lack clarity (e.g., young children may refer to sexual acts in terms of elimination rather than sexual functions, because this reflects their primary experience). (2) Essential details of the sexual activity may be left out, resulting in a disjointed, disorganized account and events may be connected in an illogical (at least to adults) manner. (3) Children may also have been told they are to blame or that the sexual behavior is beneficial or desirable, and this may result in considerable confusion for the child. (4) Children may tell different things to various people at different times because of differences in the communication styles of the adults, the types of questions asked, or simply because their memories are less well organized than those of older children or adults.

In evaluating the child's responses to the interview, the clinician must also attend to the nature of the behavior (if any) described by the child. Children often describe touching (even genital touching) that is not necessarily sexually motivated on the part of the alleged perpetrator (Berliner & Conte, 1993). The case of the 3-year-old who said his father "poked" his bottom is a good example. Another example involved a single father with limited knowledge of appropriate parenting practices who used a rectal thermometer to take the temperature of his 2-year-old daughter. The child later told her mother that "Daddy stuck a pen in my bottom," and the mother promptly filed charges of sexual abuse against her ex-husband.

In addition to evaluating the possibility of a false report of sexual abuse, the clinician must consider whether the child is intentionally distorting the truth. Although most fictitious reports of sexual abuse are thought to be the result of misinterpretations on the part of parents and clinicians, cases of intentional fabrication do occur (Berliner & Conte, 1993). Ceci and Bruck (1993) reviewed research into the conditions under which children could be induced to tell a lie and identified several different motivations including: (1)

to avoid punishment; (2) to sustain a game; (3) to keep a promise; (4) for personal gain; and (5) to avoid embarrassment; and (6) to protect a loved one.

The child's interview data must be reviewed in the context of the history of the child and family, the child's developmental status, and the circumstances surrounding the allegation of abuse. This step is particularly important for cases in which there also are issues of divorce, custody, and visitation because rates of false allegations of abuse are higher among these families than among intact families (33% vs. 5–8%, respectively) (Everson & Boat, 1989; Thoennes & Tjaden (1990).

Finally, and perhaps most important, the clinician must recognize that sometimes it is not possible to determine what, if anything, has happened and must be willing to accept this. There are two types of cases that increase the probability of an improperly conducted assessment and questionable conclusions based on the assessment data. First, some children are referred for evaluation of abuse who have in fact not been abused. Second, some children have been abused but for various reasons will not admit that it has happened. Unfortunately, it is very difficult to distinguish between these two types of cases. Clinicians may be well intentioned in attempting to persuade a child to disclose abuse (motivated by a desire to protect the child), yet to persist in pressuring a child to disclose abuse in the face of denial, greatly increases the risk of a false "disclosure" when the child has not been abused. In these cases when the clinician is uncertain about the occurrence of abuse, the child's safety must be considered in relation to the needs of the family and the suspected perpetrator. Organizing the background information collected according to the risk factors shown in Table 4.3 is helpful in negotiating a reasonable plan with child protective services for protection of the child and family. This plan should include provisions for sexuality education and abuse prevention for the child and information for the family on the potential effects of sexual abuse. In cases where the family has many risk factors, recommendations regarding treatment or monitoring by social services may be warranted.

In summary, it should be apparent that assessment in cases of alleged sexual abuse is an extremely complex process. Although we believe that a "scientist–practitioner" perspective is appropriate for all clinical work, it is most critical in sexual abuse cases. The clinician must be knowledgeable about the research on children's testimony and must be able to apply these findings to individual cases. Further, as Berliner and Conte (1993) state the clinician must recognize "that mental health professionals have no special capacity to determine whether someone is being truthful" (p. 121) and that "there is no mechanism for establishing the absolute truth, whereby it is known for sure whether or not the child was actually abused'' (p. 113). Fundamentally, the judgment that a child has or has not been sexually abused is just that—a clinical judgement. We would hope that this clinical judgment is based on the use of a systematic process for data collection and evaluation that is informed by relevant clinical and empirical work.

Treatment of Sexual Abuse

Children who have been sexually abused are a heterogeneous group and as a result, no single treatment protocol is appropriate for all of them. The clinical and empirical literature clearly indicates that children's short- and long-term reactions to abuse vary greatly and that there is no cluster of symptoms unique to sexual abuse. In addition, the potential effects of sexual abuse, and consequently the salient treatment issues, depend on the developmental level of the child. Thus, each child and family must be assessed for their ability to cope with the stressful event so that treatment can be focused on their unique needs. In this chapter, we first review different models that can be used to organize the enormous amount of information that typically is associated with these cases and to plan and guide treatment. Next, treatment issues including case management, foster care, and effective treatment methods are discussed, followed by a description of specific individual and group treatment approaches. Finally, a format for short-term treatment is presented that helps in the immediate crisis of disclosure and provides information on the need for further treatment.

MODELS FOR TREATMENT PLANNING

Given the many factors that must be considered in planning and carrying out a treatment program for sexually abused children and their families, it is helpful for the clinician to have a framework in which to organize the data gathered on the individual child and family. Such a framework can set the stage for (1) determining the importance of different contributing factors; (2) prioritizing the focus of treatment; (3) selecting treatment procedures and techniques; and (4) evaluating the effectiveness of particular treatment methods. We have found three models to be particularly helpful in our work, the traumagenic factors model proposed by Finkelhor and Browne (1985), the risk factors model by Walker et al. (1988), and the coping model developed by Friedrich (1990).

Finkelhor and Browne's (1985) model is based on four factors that help explain how children cognitively process the diverse features of sexual abuse and thus show a range of emotional and behavioral responses. The four factors are betrayal, stigmatization, traumatic sexualization, and powerlessness. Although there is not yet an empirical basis for this model, we have found it to be particularly helpful in understanding the child's perceptions of the abuse experience and the resulting symptoms. Later in the chapter we will review these four factors and show how they can help guide the child's individual treatment.

A model outlined by Walker et al. (1988) takes a broader view in considering the factors that can impact on the response to sexual abuse of the child and family. This model uses risk factors identified by research as associated with the child's adjustment to sexual abuse. The characteristics of the abuser, nonabusing family member(s), child, social, and situational context are assessed according to their degree of risk (none, mild, moderate, or severe) for a particular child, and these data are used to identify and plan interventions in each area. We have found this model particularly helpful in identifying the issues that will have to be addressed within the family and its social system. This model is outlined in Table 4.2.

Friedrich's (1990) model is based on the principles of *coping* (how one actively adapts to a stressful event or series of events and factors that enhance the ability to cope) and *human ecology* (events are embedded in various social relationships). It emphasizes four areas: (1) the functioning of the child and family prior to the abuse, including the risk and protective factors present at that time; (2) the nature of the sexual abuse; (3) the response of the child, family, school, social services, and court to the discovery of the abuse; and (4) the factors that could contribute to a "sleeper effect" or delayed onset of behavioral and emotional symptoms. This model recognizes that coping is an active process that can be influenced positively or negatively by many personal, social and environmental variables. For children, factors that can increase the ability to cope include the child's disposition or temperament, family cohesion and warmth, and an external social support system. Consideration of these factors helps the clinician understand why some children are more or less affected by sexual abuse than others and identifies areas on which to focus treatment. Each of these models can contribute to the clinician's understanding of the different behavioral and emotional responses exhibited by sexually abused children. Any one, or a combination of models, may be helpful in guiding the treatment process. We find Finkelhor and Browne's model particularly helpful, for example, in planning the child's individual treatment, while Walker et al's. and Friedrich's models are more useful in determining where to intervene in the family and environment.

TREATMENT ISSUES

It has been estimated that only 13% of children who have been sexually abused ever receive treatment (Alter-Reid, Gibbs, Lachenmeyer, Sigal, & Massoth, 1986)! Yet, the need for treatment for most children should be readily apparent. In addition to the negative effects that result from the abuse, the interventions of service systems can actually exacerbate children's problems. Further, for many children, the disclosure of abuse results in significant and traumatic disruptions in family life and daily routines at a time when the child most needs stability and support. Treatment of abused children in the absence of attention to family and environmental factors is unlikely to be effective. We have found that consideration of issues of case management and the experience of foster care to be extremely important in many cases.

Case Management

Treating children who have been sexually abused usually involves collaboration with a variety of other professionals and community agencies. Failure to consider the involved system(s) can lead to many problems including duplication of services, confusion for the family, unnecessary delays in legal proceedings, and even a lack of progress in the child's treatment. Thus, child clinicians often find themselves in the role of case manager. This critical role involves several components, including: (1) assessing the needs of the child and family through a careful review of the information that has been gathered by the professionals and/or agencies involved in the case; (2) providing information about and coordinating services for the family; (3) consulting with other professionals (e.g., police, protective services workers, district attorneys, school personnel) involved with the child and family; and (4) periodically reevaluating the family's status and needs.

Case management is often a difficult and thankless task, but professionals involved in treating sexually abused children and their families must be willing to help the family access the appropriate resources so that they can cope more effectively with this traumatic event.

Foster Care

Despite the fact that most professionals advocate for removal of the abusing family member rather than the child, between 11 and 42% of sexually abused children are removed from the home following disclosure of the abuse (Pellegrin & Wagner, 1990). The reasons for removing a child from home are diverse. In a review of protective service records, Pellegrin and Wagner (1990) found that the bases for this decision (in order of decreasing importance) included: mothers' noncompliance with a treatment program, mothers' disbelief of the child's report, the severity of the abuse, mothers' lack of employment, and the frequency of abuse. Mothers' unemployment was found to be a particularly important factor. The authors posit that unemployed mothers are financially dependent on the perpetrator and thus are not likely to support the child's disclosure. In addition to the above reasons, poor parenting skills contribute to the removal of the child. Lie and McMurtry (1991) found that over 50% of the parents whose sexually abused children were removed exhibited this deficit.

Other work characterizes the nature of the child's experience in foster care. Lie and McMurtry (1991) reviewed protective service records for 110 children who were placed in foster care after having been sexually abused by a family member. They found that 88% of these children were female with a mean age of 12.9 years. Most of the children (88%) changed placement at least once, had on average 4.8 placements, and were in the foster care system for over two years! Of those children who exited the foster care system, only 27.3% had planned reunification with the family. Although the authors indicated that the children who were sexually abused fared better in the foster care system than children who were in the system for other reasons, these data do not inspire confidence that removing a child from the home is necessarily in the child's best interest. Although it is often difficult to include parents in the treatment of children who have been sexually abused, the importance of doing so seems apparent because it is only in this way that foster care placement can be avoided or time limited. Indeed, many suggest that legal sanctions should be used more widely to ensure that parents cooperate with the child's treatment.

Research on Treatment Effectiveness

In an extensive review of outcome studies of psychotherapy with sexually abused children, O'Donohue and Elliott (1992) found only 11 empirically based studies. Unfortunately, because of a variety of methodological problems, none of the studies could definitively demonstrate the efficacy of any treatment method. Given the scarcity of empirically based studies, however, a brief review of the general conclusions that were derived from this research seems appropriate. In general, behavioral and cognitive–behavioral interventions with the children were most effective. The focus of these interventions was on increasing skills such as assertion, socialization, anxiety management, anger control, moral reasoning, academics, problem solving, and communication.

The importance was stressed of including abuse prevention training as part of any treatment program for sexually abused children, not only to decrease revictimization, but also because of the secondary benefits that such training can provide in other areas (e.g., increasing self-esteem and decreasing fears). Given the impact that their functioning has on the child, involving the parents as change agents, as well as providing treatment for the parents' own issues also was seen as a necessary part of treatment.

Treatment strategies used to treat a wide variety of behaviors in sexually abused children can successfully be adapted from programs that have been effective in treating similar symptoms due to other causes. For example, techniques such as stress innoculation training, systematic desensitization, and education that helps children "normalize" their emotional and behavioral reactions are advocated for the treatment of anxiety (Saunders, 1993), which, along with depression, was the most common symptom targeted for treatment in O'Donohue and Elliott's (1992) review.

As an example of one effective behavioral program, O'Donohue and Elliott (1992) report a study by Downing, Jenkins, and Fisher (1988) that compared psychodynamic therapy (parents and children worked on relieving guilt and increasing self-esteem) and reinforcement therapy (parents worked primarily on child-rearing issues). Treatment was conducted by therapists in the community for 22 children between the ages of 5 and 11 years. One year after treatment, parents in the reinforcement group reported that improvement had occurred 6 to 8 weeks after the start of treatment (vs. more gradual improvement for the psychodynamic group). Further, only 20% of parents in the reinforcement group felt that their children would be adversely affected by the abuse for life compared to 100% of parents in the psychodynamic group. The children in the reinforcement group also demonstrated fewer problems in specific areas (e.g., sleep, toileting, negative behavior) compared to the psychodynamic group. However, sexual self-stimulating behavior continued to be a problem for all children in both groups. Although this study did not use a controlled experimental design, the effectiveness of the behavioral versus the psychodynamic treatment was impressive.

Studies of the efficacy of group treatment suggest that short-term, structured group experiences using social learning principles can be beneficial for sexually abused children, especially school-aged children and adolescents (Corder, Haizlip, & DeBoer, 1990; Hoier, Inderbitzen-Pisaruk, & Shawchuck, 1988). Burke (1988, cited in O'Donohue & Elliott, 1992), for example, reports significant reductions in depression, anxiety, and fears for children and parents following a 6-week program that was based on social learning theory. Components of treatment included relaxation exercises, education, increasing positive reinforcement through fun activities, and role-plays to teach preventive skills. Rust and Troupe (1991) also reported significantly improved self-esteem and school achievement for 25 girls, ages 9 to 18 years, 6 months after a minimum of 6 months of group treatment. The authors used a group treatment program that encouraged honest expression of feelings, ventilation of anger, socialization training, support for court appearances, and weekly reports of day-to-day functioning from each member.

TREATMENT APPROACHES

The preceding review indicates that treatment should recognize the importance of the conditions that existed before the abuse occurred, the response of the family and the social–legal systems to the discovery of abuse, and the skills that the family and child need to cope with the sexual abuse and its consequences. The specific focus of treatment and choice of techniques will be determined by the needs of the individual child and family. Although treatment has primarily focused on the child, the importance of a multifaceted approach including individual and group treatment for both child and parent(s), as well as family therapy, cannot be overemphasized.

Individual Child Treatment

A developmental perspective is essential in treating children who have been sexually abused. Developmental factors influence all aspects of treatment, including the effects of abuse and prognosis for treatment, treatment issues and approaches, placement and protection decisions, and expectations for the child as a witness in legal proceedings. Because children understand their world differently at different ages, their understanding of sexual experiences is a function of their developmental level and will change as they develop new cognitive abilities. Thus, a sexually abused child will probably "reprocess" his or her experience of sexual abuse as cognitive capacity increases. Furthermore, developmental issues interact with treatment issues. Trust, for example, is a critical developmental issue for preschoolers and is likely to be a focus of treatment for this age group, whereas issues involving interpersonal and intimate relationships are more important for adolescents.

Our approach to treatment is structured and directive, focusing on helping children understand the abuse, develop or enhance age appropriate coping skills, and get "back on track" developmentally. We base our individual child work on a developmental approach to Finkelhor and Browne's (1986) four primary treatment issues for children: traumatic sexualization, stimatization, betrayal of trust, and powerlessness. These issues, along with related treatment strategies, are discussed in this section. The reader is referred to Table 5.1 which outlines specific intervention strategies for each of these issues at different ages.

Betrayal of Trust

Loss of a sense of security and trust in people is a significant problem when the perpetrator is a family member or other familiar person. Preschoolers, especially, have the expectation that they will be cared for and protected by adults, and this expectation is betrayed when an adult exploits them. A young child may also feel betrayed by other family members as well as by the perpetrator. For example, a 5-year-old girl who was abused by her uncle expressed intense feelings of having been betrayed by her parents because they had failed to protect her. Betrayal of trust can result in an impaired ability to judge the trustworthiness of others; some children become indiscriminately and overly attached to adults, while others show pervasive mistrust of adults and discomfort in close relationships. Significant depression, hostility, aggression, and delinquency can also result from betrayal of trust.

Treatment for this issue will vary, depending on the age of the child. Preschool children need reassurance that they will be safe, and concrete demonstrations of security such as regular routines, a nightlight, a security blanket, being allowed to cling to parents for a while, and so on. Older children can benefit from practicing problem-solving and decision-making skills in regard to specific problematic situations. Making a list of people who can be trusted and talking about when they can be trusted is another helpful activity for older children. In group treatment, "trust exercises" are fun and effective.

Stigmatization

Children who have been sexually abused often feel that they are different or stigmatized in some way. This results from an abuser blaming a child, making him or her feel like "damaged goods." A child also often feels guilty for causing the disruptions to the family that may result from the disclosure. The behavioral manifestations of stigmatization include poor self-esteem, withdrawal from social interactions and isolation from peers, and (in adolescents) delinquent activity, drug or alcohol abuse, and/or suicide attempts.

The clinician can help children identify and clarify their feelings of guilt or responsibility by pointing out when these feelings are appropriate and when

Table 5.1 Treatment Issues and Intervention Strategies for Sexually Abused Children

Age group	Traumatic sexualization	Stigmatization	Betrayal of trust	Powerlessness
0–6 years	Sex education Limits on sexual acting out Reinforcement of appropriate interactions Role-plays	*Something Happened to Me* (Sweet, 1981) Reinforcement of positive characteristics Group treatment	*Key issue*[a] Setting and keeping routines Reinforcement of independence Provide safe environment	Treatment of nightmares and sleep problems Prevention skills "What if" exercises Role-plays Identifying feelings
7–11 years	*Key issue*[a] Sex education Cognitive–behavioral techniques for assertiveness training and gaining control Reinforcement of age appropriate sexual behavior Social skills training	*Key issue*[a] *No More Secrets* (Wachter, 1983) *Liking Myself* (Palmer, 1977) Group treatment Age-appropriate activities	Making a book—"Whom can I trust?" Cognitive restructuring for depression Teaching problem-solving skills regarding trust issues	*Key issue*[a] Prevention skills "What if" exercises Assertiveness training *The Mouse, The Monster and Me* (Palmer, 1977) Letter to abuser Channeling aggression Relaxation training for fears Support success in school activities
12–18 years	*Key issue*[a] Sex education Cognitive–behavioral techniques for assertiveness training and gaining control Role-plays of relationship skills Social skills training Relaxation training	*Key issue*[a] Group treatment Age appropriate activities	Cognitive restructuring for depression Group trust exercises Using problem-solving skills regarding trust issues Listing of people who can be trusted and why	*Key issue*[a] Prevention skills Assertiveness training Letter to abuser Role-plays of relationship skills Support success in school activities Support independence

[a]*Key issue* means that this is a significant treatment issue for a particular age group.

they are not. Although a child is never responsible for the abuse, some guilt feelings may be realistic if, for example, the child was placed in a favored position by the perpetrator and then used that status to manipulate others in the family. Building self-esteem by identifying and reinforcing the child's competencies is also an important focus for treatment of stigmatization. Group treatment is especially effective in dealing with issues of blame and reponsibility, as well as isolation from peers. Group discussions can concretely demonstrate that sexual abuse happens to other children, that others may have similiar feelings about the abuse, and group members can reinforce the assignment of blame to the perpetrator, where it rightly belongs. Books such as *No More Secrets for Me* (Wachter, 1983) or *Something Happened to Me* (Sweet, 1981) can help assign responsibility for the abuse to the perpetrator. It has also been suggested that a child who is experiencing particular difficulty with feelings of being different be taken to a public place and asked to point out other people who have been abused (M. Everson, personal communication, November 16, 1988). Because this is impossible to do without talking to the people, the message is dramatically clear to the child that others cannot know he or she was abused. Finally, social skills training is effective for socially isolated children, and they (and their parents) can be encouraged to participate in age appropriate groups and activities.

Traumatic Sexualization

Traumatic sexualization refers to the distortion of the child's normal sexuality by experiences of abuse. A perpetrator of abuse often reinforces a child for inappropriate sexual behavior, or pays inordinate attention to and distorts the importance of sexual parts of the child's body. Misconceptions about sexuality and morality are also often conveyed to the child. Moreover, if the abuse involved violence, sexuality may become associated with fear and anxiety or pain. The child's sexuality is likely to be more distorted when the abuser attempts to arouse sexual responses in the child or entices the child to participate actively, and when the child is older and has a greater understanding of the implications of the abuse. The manifestations of traumatic sexualization include sexual acting out (e.g., preoccupation with sexual matters, promiscuity, compulsive sexual behavior), confusion about sexual orientation (especially for boys when the abuser is a male), distorted views of normal sexuality, or active avoidance or fear of sexual matters.

Treatment of traumatic sexualization should involve sex education, including information about what is normal sexual activity at different ages. Parents are often confused about what constitutes normal sexual behavior in children and may also need basic sex education. We have found the series of books by Sol Gordon (listed in the reference section) to be excellent resources for sex education. Parents should be helped to set limits on inappropriate sexual behavior, and the therapist should do the same during the treatment sessions. This can be done at the same time that the child's natural curiosity is satisfied (by reading a sex education book, looking at pictures, etc.). Cognitive behavioral strategies such as cognitive restructuring or thought stopping can be helpful for children who have obsessive thoughts about sex. Acceptable means of obtaining affection and attention can be taught using behavioral techniques, such as shaping, modeling, and reinforcement. Appropriate child–child and child–parent interaction can be role-played in regard to issues of friendship, affection, and caregiving.

Powerlessness

Feelings of vulnerability and powerlessness result from the child's inability to stop the abuse and are reflected in symptoms of anxiety and depression. These feelings can be exacerbated if the disclosure of the abuse is not believed or if the child is not informed about decisions being made regarding the case (e.g., whether the child will have to go to court, whether or when the child will be allowed to return home, the status of the perpetrator, etc.). Feeling a lack of control can result in excessive fears, nightmares, eating and sleeping disturbances, depression, and (in adolescents) running away and truancy. Some children will also attempt to molest other children sexually as a way of regaining control. The demonstrated vulnerability of abused children to revictimization is thought to be a result of these intense feelings of loss of control and powerlessness.

Treatment of powerlessness must involve finding appropriate ways for the child to regain a sense of control. Training in personal safety skills, including role-playing "what if" situations, is one strategy we have found effective with most children, particularly in the context of group treatment. Children can be asked to generate various strategies to deal with future abuse attempts, and then to evaluate which are safe and which are risky. The group leader can also present self-protective and nonprotective vignettes that the children can evaluate. Assertiveness skills training is also effective, especially with older children. Younger children can be allowed to choose some of the activities included in their treatment sessions and can control the stucture of the session ("We have four things to do today; which would you like to do first?"). Sleep disturbances and fears should be treated as for any child (Schroeder & Gordon, 1991).

Parent and Family Treatment

Involvement of parents and siblings, whenever possible, is a crucial part of effective child treatment. Siblings may also have been abused, and even if they have not, are likely to be confused and upset by the discovery of abuse. Their understanding of the situation can help them deal with this traumatic event more effectively. Sgroi (1982) provides suggestions for including siblings in the treatment process. The reader also is referred to Friedrich (1990) for an in-depth review of treatment with families.

Sexual abuse is fundamentally a relationship problem. Thus, a major focus of treatment of sexual abuse involves correcting failed adult–child relationships and, in instances of incest, failed relationships that span generations. Friedrich (1990) points to the influence of the mother–child relationship on the child's ability to cope with stress. Thus, it should not be surprising that the mother's response to the disclosure of abuse and her ability to support the child has a major impact on both the short- and long-term effects of the abuse on the child. Parent work in cases of incest is necessarily somewhat different than in cases involving extrafamilial abuse, and we will give a brief overview of the important issues to consider in planning treatment for these two types of cases.

In cases of *incest,* the nonabusing parent, usually the mother, is often (overtly or covertly) blamed for collusion with the perpetrator, which can set the stage for a negative attitude on the part of the clinician toward the mother, and consequently, decrease her involvement in the therapeutic process. Friedrich (1990) clearly states the need for therapists to take a neutral attitude toward mothers. They must be willing to understand the abuse from her perspective in order to help her cope with the situation. Factors that have been found to help parents cope with stress, include social support, access to financial resources, problem-solving skills, good morale, a specific belief system that is positive yet realistic, good physical and mental health, and energy. In addition to focusing on these areas, work with parents should include helping them understand what to expect as their child begins to cope with the abusive experience. The book *Helping Your Child Recover from Sexual Abuse* (Adams & Fay, 1992) is an excellent resource. In addition, helping parents provide a safe, consistent, and predictable environment for the child is a difficult but important part of this work. In instances in which the child has ongoing contact with the perpetrator or the perpetrator acknowledges the abuse, a series of family meetings (including the perpetrator) should be held to set some ground rules for appropriate and inappropriate touching, to provide ongoing support for the child, and to monitor the situation over an extended period of time.

In cases of *extrafamilial abuse,* the clinician is still dealing with an adult–child relationship problem, but the parents are not likely to be dealing with the stress of the disintegration of the family and thus, are usually more available to support the child. Friedrich (1990) points out, however, that sexual abuse usually is not a random event, and therefore, even in cases not involving incest, something sets the stage for the abuse to occur. It may be that the mother also has been abused, or that the parents were careless in making childcare arrangements, or neglectful in monitoring the child's safety and well-being. Parents will need help in dealing with their guilt feelings regarding the child sexual abuse, particularly if they have been abused themselves or have inadvertently contributed to the abuse in some way.

Group Treatment

Group treatment for both children and parents has been empirically demonstrated to be effective. Moreover, clinical experience indicates that the opportunity to share details of the abuse and receive support-confirmation of their feelings from others is important. In a description of group treatment issues with sexually abused preschool children, Damon, Todd, and MacFarlane (1987) describe a structured and directive treatment program consisting of parallel groups for preschool children and nonabusing parents. When needed, individual therapy for the child and parent is offered in conjunction with the group work. They argue that verbally oriented therapy or nondirective play therapy is not likely to be effective with preschoolers because: (1) they are not cognitively advanced enough to understand what happened to them or the motives of the adults who are trying to help them; (2) their verbal abilities are limited; and (3) the nature of sexual abuse is likely to induce "secret-keeping" and the use of denial and repression, which are primary defenses for young children; thus, these children would be unlikely to talk about the abuse without direction.

In their group treatment program, Damon et al. (1987) focus on (1) denial and repression (children deny things they wish to avoid); (2) retraction (children change their responses based on adults' reactions); (3) abandonment (separation is a genuine threat); (4) illogical beliefs (the child caused the abuse and the consequences of it); (5) sex play and sexual acting out (common behavior for this age but can be exacerbated by sexual abuse); (6) sexual knowledge (children's normal lack of knowledge is often further limited by repressive attitudes of parents); (7) regression (allows children to take the child role in a safe place); (8) fantasies about the perpetrator (children feel responsible for what may have happened to the perpetrator); and (9) assertion (children are overly eager to please adults). Treatment strategies include sex education, personal safety skills, telling the child what happened to the pepetrator, and talking openly about the abuse. They also emphasize the need to help parents understand the child's perception of the abusive event and support the changes that occur during treatment (e.g., the child freely talks about sexual matters).

Berliner and Ernst (1984) describe a group treatment program for school-aged children that uses a combination of discussion, education, games, and art activities to deal with issues of sexual abuse. Each of six sessions begins with a snack and a reminder of why the children are in the group (e.g., "You are all here because someone has touched you in a way that was wrong"). Next each child tells of a pleasant event that happened during the past week and this is followed by an art activity (e.g., making name tags, offender pictures, self-portraits, family drawings, or a group mural). Next, the leaders conduct a discussion of a topic related to abuse (e.g., what is sexual abuse, feelings about abuse, personal safety skills, etc.). A group exercise or game ends each session.

Group treatment is the treatment of choice for adolescents and would be similiar to the Berliner and Ernst (1984) format with school-aged children, but the activities would be geared to the adolescents' stage of development. Ongoing groups are particularly helpful so adolescents can leave and return periodically as needed (see Blick and Porter (1982) for more information on groups for adolescents).

FORMAT FOR IMMEDIATE SHORT-TERM TREATMENT

Providing immediate help for a sexually abused child, so that he or she can begin to understand and deal with the abuse, is crucial to the child's adjustment. Unfortunately, for many reasons, the majority of children never receive treatment or do not receive help for months after the abuse. In the hope of encouraging more clinicians to work with these children, we have developed a protocol to provide immediate and potentially time-limited treatment for children and adolescents who have been sexually abused (Schroeder & Gordon, 1991). The protocol covers many of the critical treatment issues and helps the clinician determine the need for long-term treatment. This approach is summarized in Table 5.2. Although, we have found all the components to be essential, the order in which they are included in treatment (with the exception of the first two components) is not fixed. Furthermore, the number of treatment sessions can vary depending on the needs of the individual child. It usually takes six to eight sessions, but we have done it all in one marathon session

Table 5.2 Format for Short-Term Treatment when Sexual Abuse is Substantiated

Setting the stage

1. Gather *all* background information before starting (department of social services, district attorney's office, medical records). Know family composition, child's environment and living arrangements. Determine circumstances surrounding discovery of abuse, including who substantiated it, mother's initial response.
2. Obtain estimate of child's developmental level in cognitive, emotional, social, and physical areas, in order to gear work to that level.
3. Obtain information on parent functioning. Use self-report questionnaires if information is limited.

Initial interview

1. Acknowledge abuse with parents and/or other important people (e.g., social worker, siblings) in child's presence. Reassure child regarding abuse.
2. Establish a relationship by taking time, allowing parent to be present, having enjoyable activities, and talking to child about interests.
3. Further assessment of developmental level of child if needed. Assessment of parenting skills and parent psychopathology.

Steps for treatment

1. Assess sexual knowledge of the child. Assess the family's attitudes, behavior, and beliefs regarding sexuality. Determine what and how sexuality information is shared with child. Provide appropriate sexuality education.
2. Assess knowledge of feelings and coping skills. Talk about thoughts and feelings. Teach coping skills.
3. Teach personal safety skills.
4. Include parent (or primary caregiver) in all aspects of treatment. Parents need information and support. Parenting skills also often are needed. These sometimes must be taught before sexual abuse is dealt with, or they can be taught simultaneously with the child's treatment.
5. Prepare for court if necessary.

Indicators of need for long-term treatment

1. Duration and severity of abuse, including penetration, use of force, injury
2. Parental denial of abuse
3. Parental psychopathology
4. Environmental instability, foster care placement
5. Preexisting or concomitant emotional or behavioral problems

when we had only one opportunity to see the child. It is important to note that *this treatment format is only recommended for children whose sexual abuse has been substantiated.* A brief discussion of treatment of children in cases in which abuse has not been substantiated but in which there is ongoing concern about abuse (by parents or child protective agencies) will be presented in a separate section.

Setting the Stage

Before any treatment is begun, a comprehensive assessment should be completed. The reader is referred to Chapter 4 for a complete discussion of assessment issues. It is important to gather all the relevant background and clinical information on both the parent(s) and child. The information gathered in this first step can help the clinician plan the first contact with the child and family, as well as make decisions about who to see, what questions to ask, what materials to have available, and how much case management is needed.

Initial Interview

The child and primary caregiver are usually seen together for the initial interview. If the child is in foster care, the protective service worker also often accompanies the child and should be included in the interview. Depending on the circumstances of the abuse and the status of the case, the perpetrator might also be involved in this interview (e.g., in the rare case where the perpetrator has admitted to the abuse and is willing to be involved in treatment). The primary purpose of the initial contact with the child and family is to develop rapport with the child. The clinician should explain his or her understanding of why the child and family have come to the clinic, and describe what will happen in the session. Then the parent or other caregiver is asked to tell the details of the abuse in the child's presence (children often like to play with a toy, draw, or hold a stuffed animal as they listen), while the child is periodically asked for confirmation. This serves to openly acknowledge the abuse without placing demands on the child, and allows the clinician to begin to provide the child with important information and reassurance ("Other children have told me that this has happened to them"; "It's okay to talk about it"; "You were very brave to tell," etc.). Having the parent describe the abuse in front of the child also takes the "secrecy" out of the abuse so that the parent and child can discuss it more freely with each other. At this time, the clinician can also briefly discuss the parents' or caregiver's concerns, but it should be communicated to the child that he or she is the most important focus of the session. When possible, having a therapist for both the child and parent present at this initial session allows for their individual needs to be more fully met. If this is not possible, it is important to arrange another time to talk specifically with the parents to discuss their concerns, how they might support the child, and what they might expect from their child.

Making the child feel important and in control is a primary goal, so the clinician should take considerable time to talk about the child's interests and activities, play games, draw, and have fun. Use of reflective comments and praise instead of asking many questions is essential to making the child feel comfortable. One way of communicating to the child that he or she is an important, valued person is for the clinician to keep all contracts and appointments consistently, and on time. For example, if you tell the child that she can have a snack at the end of the session or that next time you will remember to bring drawing material, be certain that you keep these promises. Although the parent or caregiver is invited to stay in the room if the child wishes, the clinician must be careful not to let the adult monopolize the session. Before the child and parent-caregiver leave, they should be told what to expect in the next session and both should be given the clinician's card in the event that either needs to call before the next session.

Issues for Treatment

The following issues are those that we feel are most important to cover with every child who has been abused, regardless of the nature of the abuse. Ideally, they are covered over a period of six to eight sessions, with parent work occurring parallel to the child's treatment. But when time is limited, the clinican will have to determine how and in what order to cover the material in the time available.

Sexual Education

Giving children information about sexuality helps them to protect themselves and results in a sense of power. We typically begin by assessing what a child already knows about normal sexuality (body parts and functions, private parts, sexual behaviors) and the terms used for sexual parts and functions. The child is then provided with appropriate information, keeping in mind that children who have been abused often have had precocious sexual experiences, and may need information that would ordinarily be more appropriate for older children. Reading a book about sexuality often elicits further questions and comments from the child and allows the clinician to provide reassurance and information directly related to the child's experience of sexual abuse. Sharing the sexual information with the parent(s) or caregiver before the session is important so that the clinician can clarify any concerns they may have about the material. It is equally important for the clinician and child briefly to review the material covered with the parent or caregiver at the end of the session. This confirms for the child that it is acceptable to talk about these things. Any concerns that the parents might have about the child's sexual behavior can be discussed at this time and plans made to handle any inappropriate sexual behavior. It is good if the sexual education materials or book used can be sent home with the child.

Feelings and Coping Skills

Children's knowledge of feelings and their ability to cope with them is dependent on their developmental status, so assessment of what they currently understand is essential prior to attempting to deal with their feelings about the sexual abuse. We often begin by making a "feelings book" in which various feelings are described and illustrated. Older children enjoy making lists of things that make them happy, sad, angry, and so on, as well as how to cope with these feelings. Younger children can cut out pictures depicting various feelings and paste them on each page. They then can be taught what to do when they feel angry, sad, afraid, and so forth. Adolescents often like to draw a picture of themselves with different feelings represented by different colors and then talk about situations that make them feel that way, as well as ways to cope with those feelings. A variety of techniques are effective in helping children deal with feelings about the perpetrator. As an example, a 6-year-old girl who was not able to talk about her feelings, demonstrated them each week in doll play. Then the clinician wrote a short story dealing with each issue to read to her the following week.

Older children often find it helpful to dictate or write a letter to the perpetrator which can be sent or not sent depending on the circumstances. Children usually want to know, and should be told what has happened to the perpetrator. The clinician should not appear surprised to hear concern or affection expressed for the perpetrator. In incest cases, the child has to be helped to understand that he or she can have both negative and positive feelings toward the perpetrator, but that the behavior of the perpetrator was wrong and not the child's fault.

Personal Safety Skills

Teaching sexually abused children self-protection skills is essential to restoring a sense of personal control and power. There are many programs available that are appropriate for group treatment. For individual work, we have found that *A Better Safe than Sorry Book* (S. Gordon & J. Gordon, 1984) is excellent for children ages 6 to 11, while *My Very Own Book About Me* (Stowell & Dietzel, 1982) is good for younger children. In addition, children (and especially adolescents) should be provided with the opportunity to practice skills in role-play situations. The importance of telling someone should be recognized and a list should be made of who the child should tell. Children also should be told that it is not their fault if they cannot get away or make someone stop hurting them. The important thing is to tell someone so that the person can be made to stop hurting the child.

Parent Work

Because the response of parents to the abuse of their children is closely tied to the children's adjustment, parent work is a central part of treatment for these children. The use of group therapy is highly recommended for parents who are dealing with the sexual abuse of a child. In many instances, parents also will need to be seen for individual therapy. In the *Short-Term Treatment Format* discussed here, parents are given basic instruction in parenting skills, or at least help in appropriately managing the behavioral sequelae of the abuse. We provide parents with information about normal sexuality and abuse prevention skills, usually sending home material used in treatment with the children. Parents who are extremely upset, to the extent that they are temporarily unable to meet their child's needs, may need separate sessions with the clinician in which they can express and work through their feelings about the abuse and receive support from the therapist. If one-way mirrors are available, allowing parents to observe their child's sessions can help them come to terms with the abuse. Finally, most parents appreciate help with the many decisions that must be made, especially if the case will be prosecuted.

Preparation for Court

Although testifying in court can be a very stressful experience for children, many children with whom we have worked have found it is actually beneficial, especially if the child's testimony is believed and the perpetrator is found guilty. Good preparation helps children and parents handle the experience as well as possible. Both parents and children need to know what to expect from a court appearance. A visit to the courtroom should be arranged some time shortly before the start of a trial; the child should be told who will be there, where these people will sit, what will happen and in what order, and what is expected of the child. In the weeks prior to the trial, the child can be prepared to testify by role-playing various situations that are likely to occur during the trial. Having the child assume a variety of roles (including those of the judge, prosecutor, and witness) helps to develop a sense of control and relieve anxiety. The actual incident of abuse under examination should not be used as content for these role-plays, lest the clinician be accused of biasing the child's testimony. For example, role-plays of the child being a witness to a car accident or of someone shoplifting could be used.

There are a few books available for children about being a witness at a trial (Anderson & Finn, 1986; Beaudry & Ketchum, 1987). We have found, however, that "homemade" books with simple line drawings that are specific to an individual child's experience are just as effective. The parent(s) and child should be aware that parents may not be allowed into the courtroom during the child's testimony. Another person who is well known and liked by the child (a teacher, family friend, neighbor, social worker, etc.) should be designated as a special support person and should sit in the front of the courtroom where the child can see him or her. The child should also be prepared for either a "guilty" or "not guilty" decision by the jury. It is likely that the child will have ambivalent feelings about a guilty verdict, especially if the perpetrator is a family member, and these feelings should be explored. In the case of a not guilty verdict, the child needs to know this does not mean that the abuse did not happen and that the clinician still believes the child.

Indicators for Longer-Term Treatment

Although the above described treatment program is sufficient for many children and provides a good starting place for most cases of sexual abuse, some children will continue to need treatment beyond the six to eight sessions. The clinician must assess the status of each child and family at the end of these sessions, taking into account factors that have been identified in the empirical literature as contributing to the need for longer-term treatment (see Chapter 3). Factors shown to be associated with poorer adjustment on the part of child victims of sexual abuse include (1) the duration and severity of the abuse (longer duration means a poorer prognosis); (2) parental denial of the abuse; (3) environmental instability; and (4) ongoing emotional, behavioral, or learning problems. Older children, and especially adolescents, are likely to need longer treatment, because they are aware of the implications of the abuse for their own developing social and sexual relationships. Furthermore, the longer the abuse has gone on, the more likely the child is to have suffered damage to self-esteem and personal identity—both key issues in adolescent development.

Similarly, abuse involving anal, oral, or genital penetration, or abuse that results in injury to the child is related to poorer adjustment.

Parents who deny the possibility of abuse in spite of a child's disclosure of abuse, or who minimize the potential negative effects, make it difficult for the child to feel accepted and safe. These parents will need help in understanding the reasons for their denial (we have found that many of these parents were themselves molested as children and have not come to terms with their own experience) and in meeting the child's needs for emotional support. The child also will need additional help in dealing with this lack of support and the poor parent–child relationship. If the parent also has significant psychopathology, especially depression (which may have been present before the abuse was disclosed) then the child is likely to need ongoing help in learning to cope with living with a dysfunctional parent.

Children who live in unstable environments, especially those who are in foster care, experience considerable stress in addition to the experience of sexual abuse and will need ongoing help in coping with these stresses. Children who have other problems that either predate or result from the abuse will need further treatment focused specifically on these problems. Finally, we have found that most children need a ''booster'' session(s) from time to time as they progress through developmental stages. With increasing cognitive skills children come to a different, more complex understanding of their experience and often have new questions or concerns about the abuse.

TREATMENT CASES INVOLVING NONSUBSTANTIATED ABUSE

The clinician often is asked to treat children for sexual abuse even though previous investigation(s) have not determined that abuse has occurred. (This work should not be confused with a referral for a second opinion on whether or not the child has been abused.) These referrals may be due to a child's inability to tell about the abuse due to age or disability, an unwillingness to disclose this information, or the fact that no abuse has occurred. The referral also can result from parental conflict, especially when heated divorce and custody proceedings are involved. A thorough review of all pertinent backgound information, including previous investigations by the legal or social service systems, other mental health professionals, and medical records, should be done prior to seeing the child (see Chapter 4 for discussion of the assessment process with these types of referrals).

In providing treatment for children for whom abuse has not been substantiated, the clinician must be very careful to take a neutral position regarding the possibility of abuse, instead focusing on the specific behaviors of concern. It is important not to repeatedly question the child about sexual abuse or use books that describe a child being abused or children being afraid to tell about abuse. These books often contain detailed information that is highly suggestible, especially to young children, and increase the risk of a false allegation. By treating the child as if he or she may or may not have been sexually abused, any disclosure that might occur during the treatment process can be viewed more objectively. In addition to treating specific child behaviors, intervention should include an assessment of the child's knowledge of sexuality, and information about sex education and personal safety should be provided to both the child and parents. It also may be important to work with the parents to determine why they are worried about sexual abuse and to consider alternative explanations for their concerns.

Many clinicians unintentionally encourage a persistent concern about sexual abuse by telling parents that although abuse cannot be substantiated, there are "red flags" that suggest that abuse could have occurred. In fact, there are no valid "indicators" for sexual abuse (Berliner & Conte, 1993). If the clinician is concerned about the possibility of abuse, his or her approach should be to help the child gain information about sexuality and personal safety in the absence of material suggesting sexual abuse. If one parent is concerned that the other parent is abusing the child, it is *critical* to include that suspected parent in the treatment process. In the presence of both child and parent, specific ground rules for appropriate and inappropriate touch should be set, the child should be instructed to tell the therapist or parents about any situations that make him or her uncomfortable, and the situation should be closely monitored for up to a year (Hewitt, 1991).

Clinicians can also put themselves in a position of "looking for abuse" in the course of treatment by not doing a thorough review of previous work with the child and family, relying solely on the information presented by the concerned parent, or aligning themselves with one parent against the other. We recently worked on a case that illustrates this clinical pitfall. Over a 2-year period two boys, ages 4 and 6, were interviewed 36 times by 13 different individuals (!) and had repeatedly denied abuse by their father. Despite this evidence, the mother took the children to a therapist who provided individual and group treatment for "sexual abuse." Although she was aware that the parents were in the middle of a heated divorce, the therapist did not review the previous work done with these children (which included a very thorough psychological evaluation of the children and both parents, indicating significant psychopathology for the mother but not for the father) nor did she ask to meet with the father. The therapist aligned herself with the mother who believed that the children were being sexually abused by their father. Her therapeutic work consisted of reading highly suggestive stories about other children having been abused, including the two children in discussions with other children in group treatment about sexual abuse, and persistent encouragement to "tell what happened to them." It was not surprising that after 10 sessions, the children "disclosed" that their father had abused them! Fortunately, abuse charges were not brought against this father, but the damage done to these children and their relationship with their father was devastating.

SUMMARY AND CONCLUSIONS

Although research evaluating the efficacy of various approaches to treatment is just beginning, many behavioral and cognitive behavioral strategies that have been shown to be effective with other clinical populations are applicable to cases involving sexual abuse. For many children, a structured directive approach is effective in addressing the most central issues in an efficient manner. Given the reality that most children receive little or no treatment, we advocate a short-term treatment approach as a first step in working with these children. This approach can set the stage for further treatment for those children who need it. Treatment of sexually abused children and adolescents can involve many pitfalls for the unwary clinician. We believe that a multifaceted approach to treatment, involving both individual and group work, is necessary to cover all the complex factors that influence children's adjustment and avoid these pitfalls. Finally, and perhaps most important, parents, even the perpetrator of the abuse in some cases, and siblings must be included in treatment whenever possible. It is unrealistic to think that children will improve if the most important people in their lives are not also involved in the process of change.

6

Sexuality and Mental Retardation

A discussion of sexual issues related to children and adolescents with mental retardation is included in this book because of the critical need to acknowledge their sexuality and to support their psychosexual development. We hope it will provide clinicians with useful information and encourage them to provide services in the area of sexuality for children and adolescents with mental retardation. This chapter includes a brief historical review of myths and attitudes about sexuality of people with mental retardation, discussion of sexual development and sexual education, and a review of the research on sexual abuse and other sexual problems, with an emphasis on assessment and treatment issues that are unique to this population.

MYTHS AND ATTITUDES ABOUT SEXUALITY AND MENTAL RETARDATION

Understanding the history of society's view of sexuality of people with mental retardation is important in placing current attitudes and practices in perspective. Although professional and societial perceptions of this special population have changed over time, resistance to or denial of their sexuality has persisted (Rhodes, 1993). In the mid-1800s moral training was seen as an important part of the education of children with mental retardation but the primary, and often the only, goal of this training was to eliminate sexual behavior. The rationale for eliminating the sexual behavior of people with mental retardation was that these behaviors were thought to contribute to the individual's disabilities or to increased incidence of mental retardation in the general population (Rhodes, 1993). Masturbation, in particular, was viewed as a debilitating behavior. This sexual behavior was thought to be contagious, leading to mental retardation not only in the person who masturbated but also in their progeny (Howe, 1976). Thus, great pains were taken to eliminate masturbation as well as all other types of sexual activity in people with mental retardation.

In the early 1900s, a distinction was made between people with mild mental retardation and those who were more severely affected. People with mild retardation were viewed as more "dangerous" to society because they were more likely to live outside of institutions, and thus to have opportunities to engage in sexual activities and possibly to have children. At this time, sterilization of people with mental retardation was widely used as a way of decreasing the incidence of mental retardation, and thus, ultimately controlling society's problems of crime and incompetence (which were thought to be largely caused by people with mental retardation). By the 1970s, more than 60,000 people in the United States were reported to have been involuntarily sterilized (Lombardo, 1982)! Fortunately, the courts have now affirmed the rights of people with mental retardation to sexual expression, and involuntary sterilization is viewed as severe and punitive (Melton & Scott, 1984). In fact, it is now difficult for people with mental retardation to be *voluntarily* sterilized, a right easily exercised by the rest of the population!

The concepts of deinstitutionalization and normalization which became popular in the 1970s and 1980s, acknowledged the individual rights of persons with mental retardation and set the stage for a shift away from the view that society needed to be protected from them (Melton & Scott, 1984). Although society now promotes the rights of persons with mental retardation to educational opportunities, employment, and life in the least restrictive environment, it has been slow to acknowledge the right to social or sexual relationships.

In general, data indicate that caregivers and parents tend to avoid discussing sexual topics with children and adolescents who have mental retardation for fear that such discussion will stimulate sexual behavior. There is even a general discomfort with the precursors of sex: tenderness, affection, and warmth expressed through touch (Craft & Craft, 1978), despite the fact that these are fundamental human needs. There are probably many reasons for these repressive attitudes, including fears of pregnancy, marriage, possible legal issues, a belief that people with mental retardation are not capable of giving informed consent to sexual experience, and a general repugnance for the idea of people with mental retardation having sexual experiences (McCabe, 1993; Murphy & Hinnes, 1994). Regardless of what lies behind repressive attitudes, it is clear that the sexuality of people with mental retardation continues to be viewed more as a problem than a positive personal attribute.

Unfortunately, there is little empirical data on the sexual lives of people with mental retardation, particularly in the United States. In the following section, the limited work that has been done on sexual development is summarized.

SEXUAL DEVELOPMENT

Physical Development

Just as for children without mental retardation, the physiology for arousal and orgasm, and the capacity for a variety of sexual behaviors begins at or before birth for children with mental retardation. However, research on the physical development of children with mental retardation indicates that they cannot be viewed as a homogeneous population. Among girls with mental retardation, there tends to be more variability in the timing of the onset of puberty than is typically found in the general population, with menarche beginning as early as 11 years, 3 months and as late as 19 years (Evans & McKinlay, 1988). Moreover, specific syndromes appear to have unique consequences for the onset of puberty, at least among girls. For example, adolescent girls with Down's syndrome have been found to reach puberty much earlier than other girls with mental retardation (Evans & McKinlay, 1988). In girls with the Prader-Willi syndrome, menarche is generally late or absent (Kauli, Prager-Lewin, & Laron, 1978) while girls with hydrocephalus, regardless of the etiology, often have precocious puberty (Tomono et al., 1983). The research on maturation of boys with mental retardation is even more limited than with girls; however, their sexual maturation does not appear to be significantly different from that of normally developing boys (Chamberlain, Rauh, Passer, McGrath, and Burket, 1984; Gebhard, 1973).

Sexual Behaviors

It is often stated that people with mental retardation have poor impulse control and thus are likely to engage in inappropriate sexual behaviors or not be able to control their sexual desires. However, when given appropriate training and opportunities for sexual expression, individuals with mental retardation engage in sexual behaviors that are similiar to those of the general population (necking and kissing) and demonstrate that they are capable of internalized self-control of their sexual behavior in both community and institutional settings (Edgerton & Dingman, 1964; Edgerton, 1973).

The expression of sexual behavior among females with mental retardation appears to be related to the level of retardation and to the setting in which the individual lives. Women with mild mental retardation who live in independent or semi-independent settings appear to engage in sexual behaviors (including intercourse) at about the same rate or somewhat less than women without mental retardation (Simonds, 1980; Timmers, DuCharme, & Jacob, 1981). Those who have more severe mental retardation have reduced rates of sexual behavior. For instance, Chamberlain et al. (1984) studied the sexual behaviors of 87 adolescent girls/young women, ages 11 to 23 years with IQs ranging from 41 to 69, who were living in community settings. Half of those with mild retardation were found to have had sexual intercourse, a proportion somewhat less than in the general adolescent population. In contrast, 32% of those with moderate retardation and only 9% of the adolescents with severe retardation had had intercourse. Forty-eight percent of those who engaged in sexual intercourse had used contraceptives. Forty-three percent of those who were sexually active became pregnant, indicating that contraceptives were either used inconsistently or not at all, or were not effective. Thus, although women with mental retardation may engage in sexual behaviors at lower rates than the normal population, they are similiar to adolescents without mental retardation in their lack of sufficient information about the implications of that behavior and in their inconsistent or ineffective use of contraceptives.

While research on the sexual behavior of males who have mental retardation is dated or limited, it suggests that when they live in the community and have access to some means of sexual expression (e.g., wives or prostitutes), they engage in similar types and frequencies of sexual behavior as men without retardation. For males who live in institutional settings, higher rates of prepubertal homosexual behavior and lower rates of premarital heterosexual contact are reported, probably due to the characteristics of the living environment (Gebhard, 1973).

It should not be surprising that people with mental retardation have the desire to marry and have children. However, society has taken a very negative attitude toward this desire, probably based on the fear that the offspring of these marriages will contribute to the incidence of mental retardation. It is true that people with mental retardation have a higher risk of having children who also have mental retardation (Hall, 1975). However, they also have a lower rate of reproduction than the general population (Craft & Craft, 1979). If both parents have mental retardation, the risk of having a child with mental retardation is 40%; if only one parent has mental retardation the risk is 15% versus a 1% risk if neither parent has mental retardation (Reed & Reed, 1965).

Thus, the issue of marriage and parenthood for people with mental retardation is complicated. Society's belief that people with mental retardation should not marry has some basis in fact. Moreover, there is a genuine concern with their ability to adequately care for children. Unfortunately, however, this attitude has greatly affected the information about sexuality that is given to people with mental retardation and has restricted their opportunities for intimate relationships despite the fact that these marriages can be successful, particularly among those with mild mental retardation, and do not necessarily have to involve child rearing (Craft & Craft, 1979; Edgerton, 1973).

To summarize, the literature that is available indicates that sexual behavior of people with mental retardation is shaped by environmental factors. When they live in a mainstream environment, their sexual behavior is similar to that of same-age peers without retardation. Conversely, when they reside in institutional settings their sexual behavior involves increased masturbation and homosexual contact. Further, when adults with mild mental retardation are allowed to express their sexuality in appropriate ways, they are, in general, competent in terms of biological capability, sexual desire, and the psychological significance they attribute to sexual behavior (Hall, 1975). However, they typically lack basic information about sexuality that would enhance their ability to engage in intimate relationships, as well as help them to be aware of the implications of that behavior and to protect themselves from exploitation.

Knowledge of Sexuality

Similar to the general population, sexual experience for people of all ages with mental retardation typically precedes knowledge and understanding (Edmonson, McCombs, & Wish, 1979; Ousley & Mesibov, 1991; Robinson, 1984). But people with mental retardation are, as a group, more heterogenous than the general population in their knowledge level. Sexual knowledge appears to be related to IQ (the higher the IQ the greater the knowledge), level of adaptive behavior, attitudes of parents and caregivers, gender (girls and boys have different information about different topics), and the nature of sex education programs targeted to the special needs of these individuals.

In an early study of sexual knowledge, Fischer and Krajicek (1974) interviewed 16 adolescents (10 to 17 years of age) with moderate mental retardation and found that these youngsters knew very little. All of them where able to identify their own gender and knew the difference between boys and girls. They were able to give colloquial but not correct anatomical names for sexual body parts. Both boys and girls had words to explain urination and bowel movements, but only 50% of the girls and very few boys understood menstruation. Only the boys had their own words to describe masturbation, but few knew the purpose of it. Everyone was able to accurately identify intimate behaviors such as hugging, kissing, and sexual intercourse, but they could not explain why people engaged in these behaviors. Likewise, they could identify pregnant women, but they did not know how one becomes pregnant or the length of the pregnancy. Surprisingly, boys had a better understanding of the birth process than did the girls. In an encouraging note, the authors indicated that the parents of the youngsters viewed their participation in this study as a very positive experience and said that it helped change their attitudes about giving information to their children and accepting that their children already had some information, even though it was often erroneous.

In a similar study, Brantlinger (1985) interviewed 13 adolescents (14 to 17 years) with mild mental retardation about their knowledge of and attitudes toward sexuality. Ten of the 13 students thought that sex was dirty and nasty. "They communicated that they had been taught not to talk about it, and most conveyed that sex was something you did on the sly though you really should not be doing it" (Brantlinger, 1985, p. 103). Although a range of knowledge was demonstrated, none of the adolescents could be described as well informed, and the majority had very little or very inaccurate information. For example, one boy stated that to have a baby "a man has to go real fast. If he wants to have two kids he has to go real, real fast" (Brantlinger, 1985, p. 103). This boy was described as one of the more "street-wise" youngsters! Only one out of the 13 believed that the purpose of sex is reproduction. Three of the participants had almost no sexual information, yet two of the three were sexually active.

Ousley and Mesibov (1991) compared interview responses of young adults with autism with those of a group of people with mild mental retardation of the same age. They found that females in both groups were more interested in dating than males, and that although people with autism expressed an interest in sexuality, they had significantly less experience than those with mental retardation. Neither group was very knowledgable about sexual topics, but IQ was a better predictor of knowledge than either experience or interest.

Taken together, these findings indicate that the sexual knowledge of adolescents with mental retardation is partial, inaccurate, inconsistent, and contains many misperceptions. The data also indicate that knowledge of sexual information typically does not increase interest in sexual issues. Rather, it can give people a better understanding of topics that are already of interest. Further, it is apparent that sex education programs must be geared to the cognitive level of the student.

SEX EDUCATION

Given that many people with mental retardation engage in sexual activities, their lack of accurate information on sexual issues puts them at increased risk for a variety of negative experiences, including unintentional pregnancy, sexually transmitted diseases, sexual abuse, and sexually inappropriate behavior. Similar to their caregivers and the general population, people with mental retardation have very conservative attitudes about sexual matters and a generally negative view of sexual behaviors (Brantlinger, 1985; Edmonson et al., 1979). This makes it very difficult for them to get information about sexuality. They are not likely to ask questions; they are not likely to be given information in a way that they can understand; and they are discouraged from expressing even the most basic need for physical contact.

Although the need for sex education should be apparent, resources for information and training to enable these individuals to manage their sexual needs and to protect themselves are limited (Huntley & Benner, 1993). Parents and teachers do not appear to be good sources of sexual education. For instance, Brantlinger (1988) discovered that fewer than half of the special education teachers in her sample included sexual education in their curriculum and those who did, did not cover the topic in depth. In addition, only half (53%) of the students reported that their parents gave them information about sexuality. Most of these students felt that this was difficult for the parents to do and that the information was not very helpful.

Given that children with mental retardation are not likely to get sexual information from parents or teachers, what are their sources of information? In the Brantlinger (1985) study, 46% of the students said that they had talked with their siblings or peers about sex. Other reported sources of information included pornographic magazines and TV. Not surprisingly, these meager resources were found to provide erroneous and incomplete information.

Because of their diverse strengths and weaknesses, it is obvious that not all people with mental retardation can benefit from sex education, and not all types of information are appropriate for all those who can benefit. However, the sequence of sexual development and knowledge for normally developing children provides a framework for teaching sexual information to children with mental retardation. Tables 1, 2, and 3 in Chapter 1 outline the information that should be considered in the sexuality education of children and adolescents with mental retardation. It is important that this infomation be presented on an ongoing basis and included as part of formal teaching about health and hygiene, decision making, problem solving, social skills, self-efficacy, and interpersonal relationships.

Prevention of sexual abuse is also a terribly important topic for children and adolescents with mental retardation. Prevention efforts should begin with programs similar to those designed for nonretarded children so that to the extent possible, appropriate and inappropriate behaviors and dangerous or exploitive situations can be discriminated. However, it must be recognized that many individuals with mental retardation are not capable of self-protection at all times and in all situations. Thus, prevention programs must be broadly focused on the environmental context in which these children live to ensure that they receive adequate supervision and protection.

A number of factors are important in planning and carrying out sexual education programs to ensure that the knowledge level is maintained and generalized. Giving parents information about the importance of sexuality in their children's lives, asking parents about their concerns, allowing them to give input on what should be taught, and giving them feedback on what is being taught, will increase the likelihood that the new skills and behaviors their children learn will be reinforced and maintained (Toomey, 1993). In addition, involving parents in the process of sex education early in the child's life is one way to change potentially negative attitudes about sexuality. Since many children with mental retardation move to residential settings as they reach adulthood, parents should be encouraged to work with these agencies to clarify the value system within the agency, and to develop an explicit policy statement and guidelines for sexual behavior (Huntley & Benner, 1993). Further, the assessment of cognitive, communication, and adaptive behavior skills, as well as a pretest of knowledge of and misperceptions about sexuality, is essential for each student before implementing a sex education program.

In general, information should be presented in a concrete and explicit manner and training should include the use of role-play, representational models of nude people, modeling of desired skills, practice using skills in a variety of situations and with a variety of people, and repetition. The opportunity to participate in groups also can be a particularly effective method with adolescents and adults with mental retardation as these people are likely to share many of the same issues and concerns. For instance, Levy, Perhats, Nash-Johnson, and Welter (1992) found that including teenage mothers with mild mental retardation in educational and support groups with younger teenage mothers without retardation promoted school attendance and increased the time between pregnancies, plus it was an effective intervention for the children of both groups of teenagers. Because people with mental retardation learn more slowly, the implementation of sex education programs must be done over extended periods of time, and it should not be surprising to find that any given program may take up to 3 years to complete (Bellamy, Clark, Hamre-Nietupski, & Williams, 1977).

A variety of sexual education programs for children and adolescents with mental retardation are available. For instance, the James Stanfield Publishing Company (PO Box 41058, Santa Barbara, California 93140; 1–800–421–6534) specializes in training materials for people with developmental disabilites and has an excellent series on sexual education. An example of another approach is a book by Shea and Gordon (1991) that is designed for individual reading and discussion. It covers important areas of sexuality in an explicit and concrete format with pictures that illustrate important concepts and simple text. The book also provides practice exercises and questions for further discussion. It is available from The Clinical Center for the Study of Development and Learning, CB No. 7255, University of North Carolina, Chapel Hill, NC 27599; 1–919–966–5171.

In summary, the need for life-long sexuality education for people with mental retardation has been well documented. Without appropriate information about this important area, they are not able to make informed choices or fully exercise their rights for sexual expression. In the past, sex education for children with mental retardation was considered when problems arose, typically in adolescence. Yet a proactive approach would seem to be more effective in the long run, both in preventing problems from occurring and in maximizing the child's potential for a full and satisfying sexual life.

SEXUAL ABUSE

Estimates of the prevalence of sexual abuse among people with mental retardation varies from rates that are similiar to the general population, to reports of 75 to 85% of women with mental retardation who live in community residential settings being sexually abused (Davis, 1989). Moreover, children and adolescents with mental retardation tend to experience more severe and chronic abuse than children without mental retardation. A study by Sobsey (1994) indicated that 67% of children 12 and younger and 53% of those 13 to 17 years who had been abused experienced 10 or more instances of sexual abuse.

The severity of mental retardation is important in interpreting the statistics on incidence and prevalence of sexual abuse. Sobsey (1994) reviewed several studies and estimated that about 25% of people with mild mental retardation were victims of sexual abuse, a rate that is consistent with that found in the normal population. In contrast, 24% of those with moderate retardation, 41% with severe retardation and 7.5% of those with profound retardation were sexually abused. The incidence of sexual abuse among individuals in each of these latter three groups was greater than that which would be expected given their distribution in the general population, and this was especially true for those with severe retardation.

There are many reasons why people with disabilities are more likely than those without disabilities to be victims of sexual abuse. Society's view that people with mental retardation are asexual, lack the sensitivity to suffer from abuse, or are less important than others, set the stage for sexual abuse. Characteristics of their disability make these individuals more vulnerable to exploition. They often respond indiscriminately to what is asked of them. Many have been trained to be compliant with a variety of caregivers and many are physically dependent on others to a great extent. Thus, they must rely on the "good will" of the caregiver not to exploit this dependent relationship. The need to be valued and accepted increases the desire to please others which, in turn, increases the risk of exploitation. Further, many people with mental retardation have difficulty judging the motivation of others. This, coupled with the fact that they often receive little or no sex education, makes it difficult for them to make good decisions about sexual matters or to recognize what is appropriate or inappropriate behavior. Even when sex abuse prevention training has occurred, they often are not told, or it is difficult for them to understand, that family members or caregivers, as well as strangers, can be sexually exploitive. Perpetrators of sexual abuse of people with mental retardation are aware of the vulnerabilities of this population, and know that the abuse is not likely to be reported, or, if it is reported, the victim is not likely to be believed (Tharinger, Horton, & Millea, 1990). Although it is common for perpetrators to blame the victim, whether or not a disability is present, society seems more willing to accept this as a defense when the victim has a disability.

Perhaps because of the nature of mental retardation, and particularly because of the increased dependence on caregiving, research indicates a different distribution of perpetrators than is found for normally developing children. Normally developing children are most likely to be abused by a relative. In contrast, Sobsey (1994) indicates that service providers are most likely to be perpetrators (41% of offenders) of abuse with those with mental retardation, followed by family friends or neighbors, natural family members, and peers with disabilities. However, these data are likely to be influenced by the living situations of the subjects. In the Chamberlain et al. (1984) study, where a significant majority of the subjects lived in the home, nearly one-half of those who were abused were victims of incest with a father, stepfather, or foster father.

Assessment of Sexual Abuse

Investigating allegations of sexual abuse is especially challenging with children and adolescents who have mental retardation. Although the alleged victim is the primary source for information about what, if anything, happened, people with mental retardation often have great difficulty responding to questions, especially questions about who, what, where, and when. Given this problem, the clinician must take the time to gather information about the factors associated with sexual abuse (shown in Table 3, Chapter 4) from a variety of sources. Further, assessment of intellectual functioning, adaptive behavior, and communication skills must be completed before drawing conclusions or making recommendations.

All of the assessment issues outlined in Chapter 4 apply to children and adolescents with mental retardation. In this section, issues that are specific to those with mental retardation are emphasized. The discussion of these issues is based on work by Sgroi (1989) and the Guidelines of the American Professional Society on the Abuse of Children (APSAC, 1990). A summary of guidelines for assessment are shown in Table 6.1. Many of the strategies outlined will be most useful with children and adolescents who have mild mental retardation, although many individuals with moderate to severe retardation also can be successfully assessed.

Purpose of the Assessment

The first step in the assessment process is to determine the professional's role, clarify the questions being asked, and let the referral source know to what extent the questions are answerable. Sgroi (1989) states that in working with children with mental retardation, a professional might be asked to do an assessment of sexual abuse as part of a law enforcement investigation, a civil protective service investigation, or an internal investigation by the agency serving the child who is suspected of being abused. Each of these three types of investigations would require a somewhat different assessment focus and would result in different recommendations. The internal investigation of an agency is particularly relevant for children and adolescents with mental retardation. It is done by an agency to determine if some aspect of the caregiving arrangements or services provided contributed in any way to the abuse. The results of an internal investigation could include recommendations for improving the agency's services by changing agency policies, providing staff training, and so forth.

Background Information

The evaluator should review all available records, including social history, psychological evaluations and IQ testing, medical records, educational records, employment history, behavioral records, and all reports of the alleged abuse. It is important to separate reports of impressions versus actual behavioral observations (e.g., ''I think'' statements versus ''I saw'' statements). In addi-

Table 6.1 Guidelines for Sexual Abuse Assessment of Children and Adolescents with Mental Retardation

General guidelines

Identify purpose of assessment
  Law enforcement investigation
  Civil protection investigation
  Internal agency investigation
Gather background information
  General medical history
  Results of medical examination
  Social history
  Results of psychological evaluations including IQ testing
  Adaptive behavior and communication skills
  Educational records
  Employment history (if any)
  Behavioral records
  Reports of the alleged abuse

Setting the stage

Choose a neutral setting
  Invite a trusted person
Arrange for video- or audiotaping
  Explain purpose of recording
  Get consent to record
Arrange for observation if possible
  Explain purpose of observation
  Get consent for others to observe

Format for first session

Establish rapport
Administer test of intelligence
  Current cognitive functioning
  Style of communication
  Receptive and expressive language abilities
  Response to different types of questions
Assess sexual knowledge and experience
  Terminology for body parts and sexual behavior

Format for subsequent sessions

Sexual abuse interview
  Use individual's terminology for sexual behavior and body parts
  Use language appropriate to the individual's level of cognitive functioning
  Begin with nondirective, general questions (elicit the most accurate responses)
  Follow with specific or either-or questions as necessary (responses less likely to be accurate)

Table 6.1   (Continued)

Defer clarification or elaboration questions
Use reflective comments to facilitate responding
Avoid positive or negative nonverbal feedback
Assess memory and suggestibility
  Ask for details of first session
  Ask specific suggestive questions about first session:
      "You remember the woman who brought you a coke the last time you were here, what was
        her name?"
      "Were the pictures I showed you green or blue?"
      "Do you remember when I tested your eyes?"
  Ask for elaboration of any incorrect responses to suggestive questions

Evaluate the assessment data

Review the background data
Review video- or audiotape
  Responses relative to questions asked
  Presence of response set
  Consistency of responses specific to abuse
Consider all possible explanations for the data

tion, it is important to interview anyone who may have been involved in reporting the abuse or who has special knowledge of the alleged victim, such as the primary caregivers.

A medical examination is important because the findings potentially can corroborate suspicions of abuse, especially for individuals who are not able to describe their experiences. The clinician must be cautious in evaluating the results of this evaluation, however. The use of medical findings (e.g., healed genital or anal lesions) in the absence of acute findings such as pregnancy or a sexually transmitted disease to substantiate abuse, is particularly problematic with people who have mental retardation because any positive findings could be explained by factors other than sexual abuse (e.g., an undetected history of vaginal infections or injuries, excessive masturbation, etc.) (Elvik, Berkowitz, Nicholas, Lipman, & Inkelis, 1990).

Setting the Stage

The assessment should be conducted in a neutral setting, away from the home or the workplace. All interviews with the alleged victim should be either audio- or videotaped. A complete record of responses is necessary to take into account the effect that the question format may have on the responses and response bias. Before recordings are made, however, the child should be told the purpose of the recordings (to be able to get a complete record), see and perhaps try out the equipment, and give written or verbal consent for the use of recording devices.

It is best to start out with a trusted person in the room with the suspected victim and evaluator. After introductions and clarification of the purpose of the interview, the trusted person should be asked to wait outside the room. Children with mental retardation are easily influenced, so it is important to have an opportunity to see them alone. The trusted person could observe through a one-way mirror, if one is available. Similar observations by involved professionals may also be indicated if this reduces the need for additional interviews. The suspected victim should be told about observers and should give consent for them to be present.

Format for the First Session

A standardized test of intellectual functioning should be administered in the first session even if one has been done recently. This provides the opportunity to develop rapport with the child while using a structured format. This procedure also gives information on the child's current cognitive functioning, style of communication, response to different question structure (e.g., open-ended questions, short answer questions, etc.), and receptive and expressive abilities. It is also a concrete observable event that later can be used to evaluate the validity of the individual's report of abuse.

Assessing for sexual knowledge of body parts and functions and sexual behavior, as well as sexual experience also is important and can be done in either the first or second session. This assessment not only gives information on what the child knows, but also the terminology used for body parts and sexual behavior. This terminology then can be used when talking about sexual issues (for examples of instruments to assess sociosexual knowledge, see Fischer et al., 1973; Wish, McCombs, & Edmonson, 1980).

Format for Subsequent Sessions

The format for subsequent sessions is based on work by Gudjonsson and Gunn (1982), Sigelman, Budd, Winer, Schoenrock, and Martin (1982), and Sgroi (1989). The information presented in Chapter 4 on interviewing children without disabilities who are alleged to have been abused also is relevant to interviewing children and adolescents with mental retardation.

The purpose of the second session (or more, as needed) is to assess memory skills, the child's general level of suggestibility, and specific details of the alleged abuse. This session should be held as soon after the first as possible, at least within a week. A few important general issues regarding interviewing people with mental retardation are these:

1. The language and interviewing approach should be appropriate to the person's level of cognitive functioning.

2. Initial questioning should be as non-directive as possible to elicit spontaneous responses. If open-ended questions are not productive, more direct questioning should follow; however, the difficulties that are present when interviewing children who are developing normally also apply to children and adolescents with mental retardation. Responses to highly specific questions must be carefully evaluated and their credibility weighed cautiously.

Sigelman et al. (1982) report that the accuracy of responses of people with mental retardation are directly related to the types of questions asked. They provide the most information in response to "yes-no" questions ("Is it raining outside today"?), yet have a significant "yes" response bias which makes the validity of answers to these types of questions highly questionable. The "either-or" question format ("Did he put his finger or his penis in you?") elicits fewer but more valid responses. But these questions risk introducing new information to the child which may later be incorporated into the report of what happened. Open-ended questions elicit the smallest amount of information ("What did we do the last time you were here?") but the accuracy rate is highest with this format. It should be noted that when following up on answers, prompts such as "What did he do then" are confusing for people with mental retardation and tend to make their responses less accurate. A better strategy is to simply repeat what the person has said.

3. Defer asking the child to elaborate or clarify responses initially, so as not to interrupt the flow of information. Reflective responses (e.g., "It sounds like you touch your private parts but you are not sure it is okay to do that"; or "It sounds like you are afraid to talk about what happened") are more likely to facilitate the discussion.

4. Because children with mental retardation tend to be very sensitive to nonverbal feedback, the interviewer must avoid communicating by tone of voice, facial expression, or body language any negative or positive response to the information given.

5. Assessing the susceptibility to suggestion is particularly important for children with mental retardation. The clinician can never assume the validity

of answers to questions in the interview; the same information must be asked for in alternative ways to determine if the answers are consistent or if there is systematic response bias (Sigelman et al., 1982). It is best to compare the responses given during the interview with an independent observation of the child's response style, and the intellectual evaluation offers this opportunity. Start by telling the child that you want to know how much he or she remembers from that session. Begin by asking general open-ended questions about what is remembered of the first session. Then ask specific suggestive questions from the following three types of formats: (1) *Questions that anticipate the answer* (e.g., "You remember the woman who brought you a coke the last time you were here, what was her name?" when no one gave her a coke); (2) *Alternative questions* (e.g.,"Were the pictures green or blue?" when, in fact, they were black and white); and (3) *Simple questions requiring a "yes" or "no" answer* but which suggest and often get an affirmative rather than a negative reply (e.g., "Do you remember when I tested your eyes?" when you did not do so). This assessment procedure will assist the clinician in making a judgment about the validity of the information about the sexual abuse incident.

Evaluating the Assessment Data

The final step in the assessment process is to evaluate the data in the context of the background information gathered. It is particularly important to list in the final report all assessment procedures, including methods of assessing suggestibility and response bias, as well as all sources of information. Probability statements about whether the abuse did or did not happen should include supporting information (e.g., the alleged victim's statements about the abuse and the questions required to elicit them, unusual behavior observed during the interview, psychological symptoms, information that is provided consistently regardless of how the question was asked, etc.).

In many cases, the evaluation may be inconclusive. If so, the clinician should describe the information that causes continuing concern but does not enable confirmation or disconfirmation of abuse. Recommendations should be made regarding therapeutic or environmental intervention to address the individual's emotional and behavioral needs and to ensure his or her safety.

Treatment of Sexual Abuse

The effects of sexual abuse and consequently the treatment issues for children and adolescents with mental retardation are not significantly different from those described in Chapters 3 and 5. Children and adolescents with mental retardation are particularly at risk for negative effects of sexual abuse because of the nature of their disability. They often have problems with poor self-esteem, social isolation, and feelings of being different, even in the absence of sexual abuse, and the experience of abuse only exacerbates these preexisting problems.

Although many psychotherapeutic techniques have not been used with people who have mental retardation, there is literature to suggest that dynamically oriented, behavioral, and play therapies, as well as individual and group therapies can be adapted to help people with mental retardation deal with psychological and emotional issues resulting from abuse (Cruz et al., 1988; Mansell et al., 1992; Matson, 1984). The approach selected and goals of therapy must take into account the person's level of understanding, ability to form relationships, and social skills, however.

We have found Finkelhor and Browne's (1985) four major treatment issues for victims of sexual abuse (traumatic sexualization, stigmatization, betrayal of trust, and powerlessness) helpful in understanding and treating people who have mental retardation.

Traumatic sexualization refers to the distortion of the person's sexuality by the experience of the abuse. This often is exhibited in confusion about sexuality, inappropriate repertoires of sexual behavior, and unusual emotional associations to sexual activities. Because an individual with mental retardation may have a history of sexual problems that predates the abuse, these problems must be taken into account in planning treatment. Treatment of sexual issues can begin with assessing knowledge and misconceptions about sexuality, and teaching appropriate and inappropriate expressions of sexuality.

Stigmatization refers to the finding that people who have been abused often feel that they are different or stigmatized in some way. Given the nature of their disability, people with mental retardation already are prone to poor self-esteem, feelings of not being valued, or of being different. The experience of sexual abuse exacerbates these negative feelings. Stigmatization is illustrated in the group treatment of eight women with mental retardation who *all* "secretly" believed that they deserved to have been abused and felt that (step)fathers had the right to molest children with disabilities but not those without disabilities (Cruz et al., 1988)! Treatment for this group included showing a film of nonhandicapped young women talking about their experiences of sexual abuse. In this way the women in the group could see that it is not just people with developmental disabilities who are abused, and that no one deserves abuse. The experience of viewing the film was reported to be a major turning point in the therapy for these women.

Betrayal of trust refers to the loss of a sense of trust and security with people on whom one depends, and is particularly significant when the perpetrator is a family member or other familiar person. Loss of trust is an especially salient issue for children and adolescents who have mental retardation. Even though they may be able to live semi-independently, most will continue to be at least partially dependent on others for their care. The women in the Cruz et al. (1988) report experienced fear that if they expressed their anger they would destroy the physical and emotional relationships upon which they were dependent. As they became more comfortable talking about their abuse, they increasingly expressed anger at the perpetrators and at their mothers who had allowed the abuse to occur or who became angry at them when told about it. One method used was to have them write letters (unsent) to their mothers and to the perpetrators during their treatment sessions. Other important components of treatment include increasing social and support networks in order to decrease dependency on caregivers or family members, and building self-confidence and feelings of acceptance through the therapeutic relationship (Cruz et al., 1988).

Powerlessness and feelings of vulnerablity reflect the person's anxiety, fear, and helplessness because he or she is or was unable to stop the abuse. People with mental retardation typically feel vulnerable and powerless, and sexual abuse further confirms these feelings. Like victims without mental retardation, feelings of powerlessness make them particularly vulnerable to repeated abuse and can also increase the likelihood that they will abuse others. Treatment of these issues must involve sexuality education and counseling on social–sexual relationships, including assertiveness and self-protection skills training. This training is particularly important for people with mental retardation given their difficulty with social perceptions and detecting the motivations of others.

Finally, case management is an especially critical component of the treatment process for children and adolescents with mental retardation who have been abused. Case management involves assessing the needs of the person across settings, assessing and developing a support network, providing information and coordinating services, consulting with other involved professionals, and reevaluating the client's status at periodic intervals.

In summary, for children and adolescents with mental retardation who have been sexually abused, the short- and long-term negative effects of the abuse are similiar to but often greater than the effects of abuse on children and adolescents without mental retardation. Issues associated with mental retardation are compounded by the effects of the sexual abuse. A wide variety of treatment approaches can be effective if they are adapted to the individual's level of understanding, ability to form relationships, and social skills. In doing this, the therapist must be willing to take the necessary time and effort to develop goal oriented treatment programs that are concrete and repetitious.

SEXUAL OFFENDERS WHO HAVE MENTAL RETARDATION

Many sexual behaviors that are considered appropriate for the general population are seen as deviant for people with mental retardation and as a result, the sexual problems reported for people with mental retardation actually may consist of normal sexual behavior. There are, however, a number of individuals with mental retardation who do engage in truly deviant sexual behavior. The literature reviewed for this section focused almost entirely on the problem of sexual deviance among adolescents with mental retardation. Many of the issues discussed, however, would be equally relevant to younger children.

In considering the problem of deviant sexual behavior in adolescents with mental retardation, it is important to determine the circumstances in which the offense occurs and to assess the nature of the behavior. Sexually deviant behavior consists of a range of behaviors, from those that violate public standards (e.g., masturbation in public, exposure of genitalia) to those that abuse other's rights (e.g., fondling, attempted or completed rape) (Schilling & Schinke, 1989). Most studies do not indicate a higher rate of sexual offenses among the developmentally disabled population than is found in the general population (Schilling & Schinke, 1989), but if a person with mental retardation is arrested the offense is likely to be sexual in nature (Murphy, Coleman, & Abel, 1983). For example, in a survey of the Washington State correctional facilities, Gross (1985, cited in Shilling & Schinke, 1989) found that nearly half of the people with mental retardation were incarcerated for sexual offenses. He also found that in state institutions for people with developmental disabilities, 21% of those convicted of felonies had committed sexual crimes.

Schilling and Schinke (1989) point out that many of the social and behavioral correlates of mental retardation are similiar to characteristics of sexual offenders (e.g., social isolation, social skills deficits, preference for the company of young children, lack of consideration for the consequences of behavior, easy access to vulnerable people). Moreover, people with mental retardation often are restricted from engaging in normal appropriate sexual behavior. These two factors taken together could contribute significantly to a higher reported incidence of sexual offenses in this population. On the other hand, circumstances that limit the participation of people with mental retardation in society (e.g., decreased opportunities to date, plus decreased mobility and increased close supervision) also decrease their opportunities to commit sexual offenses.

Comparison of characteristics of adolescents with and without mental retardation who commit sexual offenses indicates few differences. A survey by Gilby, Wolf, and Goldberg (1989) examined the extent and types of sexual problems of 196 adolescents with and without mental retardation who were patients in a psychiatric institute. They found that adolescents with and without mental retardation had similiar rates of sexual problems, with 21% of the outpatients and 40% of the inpatients reported for sexual offenses. The adolescents with mental retardation engaged in significantly more nuisance-type behaviors such as public masturbation or exhibitionism, whereas the adolescents without mental retardation engaged in more consensual but inappropriate behaviors such as having sexual intercourse in a public place. The two groups were equal in the frequency of nonconsensual or assaultive sexual behaviors such as fondling or forced intercourse. Among the differences found were that adolescents with mental retardation (1) were less discriminating in their choice of victims, choosing both male and female, child and adult, but less often knew their victims; (2) came from families with less conflict; and (3) engaged in less delinquent behavior. There were no personality characteristics that distinguished these two groups or a third group of adolescents with mental retardation who had behavioral problems but did not commit sexual offenses. Taken together, these data indicate that adolescents with mental retardation do not necessarily engage in more sexual offenses than adolescents without mental retardation. However, they do engage in more behaviors that could be the result of lack of training in discriminating appropriate from inappropriate behavior.

Assessment of Sexual Offenders

Because of the extent to which normal sexual expression by individuals with mental retardation is viewed as deviant, clinical assessment of sexual offenses in this population is complex. The assessment process is similar to that for sexual abuse and should include a complete description of the act including its nature and frequency, the age, developmental levels, and relationship of the people involved, the prevailing cultural and family attitudes about sexuality, and the exploitive nature of the behavior (Schilling & Schinke, 1989).

In attempting to distinguish truly deviant from merely inappropriate sexual behavior, Hingsburger, Griffiths, and Quinsey (1991) use the term "counterfeit deviance" to describe behavior that appears to be deviant, but upon further investigation is found to be the result of other factors. They suggest

11 hypotheses that help differentiate sexually inappropriate from sexually deviant behavior. The information gathered in assessing these hypotheses can help determine whether the behavior is inappropriate or offensive versus a true sexual offense, as well as help guide the development of a treatment plan. These hypotheses include:

1. *The Structural Hypothesis.* Because people with mental retardation usually live in settings that do not allow any expression of sexuality or privacy, maladaptive ways to deal with the system are learned. These include engaging in sexual behaviors in places or at times that staff cannot find them, such as in bathrooms or late at night. Assessment of this hypothesis involves investigation of the agency, caretakers', or parental attitudes on sexuality, as well as the opportunity for appropriate social–sexual relationships.

2. *The Modeling Hypothesis.* The increased dependency of adolescents with mental retardation often results in parents and caretakers seeing them naked or touching them in the course of dressing or bathing, and they model behaviors, therefore, that are inconsistent with the rules of privacy and modesty. Assessment of the modeling hypothesis involves examining the nature of the adolescent's interaction with the staff, as well as the opportunities for privacy.

3. *The Behavioral Hypothesis.* Given that sexual behavior is difficult to ignore, staff may inadvertently reinforce it through their negative attention to it. Negative attention is especially reinforcing if there is little stimulation in the environment or if opportunities to reinforce other more appropriate behaviors are limited. The behavioral hypothesis involves investigation of the appropriateness of daily routines and activities, opportunities for positive interactions, and consequences for appropriate and inappropriate behavior.

4. *The Partner Selection Hypothesis.* There often is such a lack of opportunities for developing age appropriate relationships that the adolescent has become inappropriately attacted to staff or children, or is too friendly to inappropriate people or in inappropriate circumstances in a desperate attempt to interact and be accepted. The opportunity to develop social–sexual relationships should be investigated to assess this hypothesis.

5. *The Inappropriate Courtship Hypothesis.* Developing social–sexual relationships is a very complex task that includes learning to discriminate between sexual and nonsexual behavior, appropriate and inappropriate interactions, and public and private behavior. The specific training provided in interpersonal relationships should be investigated as the client may be attempting to form a relationship through intrusive and inappropriate behaviors.

6. *The Sexual Knowledge Hypothesis.* It is a life-long experience to learn about one's sexuality. For people with mental retardation, this requires explicit

on-going training in sexuality to help them both understand and have the opportunity to express their sexuality in an appropriate manner. The training in sexuality that the person with mental retardation has been provided with should be investigated.

7. *The Perpetual Arousal Hypothesis.* People with mental retardation often have difficulty achieving sexual satisfaction in appropriate ways due to a lack of privacy or limited knowledge on how to reach orgasm when masturbating. This sexual ''frustration'' could lead to frequent masturbation or other sexual behaviors in public situations. The opportunity for privacy and the ability of the person to achieve sexual satisfaction should be investigated.

8. *The Learning History Hypothesis.* The history of where the adolescent has lived and the opportunities he or she has had for learning appropriate social–sexual behaviors should be investigated. If the adolescent's experience has included multibed facilities, a very protected environment, or a history of sexual abuse, he or she might not have had the opportunity to learn about societal standards regarding sexual behaviors.

9. *The Moral Vacuum Hypothesis.* Without moral training it is difficult to have an understanding and appreciation for the effect one's behavior has on other people, and, therefore, to understand the emotional and physical pain of the victim. It would be important to assess moral development and the need for training in this area.

10. *The Medical Hypothesis.* There could be a medical problem such as a urinary tract or yeast infection that is difficult for the client to report and results in what appears to be sexual activity. A thorough medical evaluation should be part of the investigation to rule out this possibility.

11. *The Medication Side-Effect Hypothesis.* Certain medications can affect sexual satisfaction and performance and it is important for the person receiving them and his or her caregivers to know of these side effects. A careful review of medications should be done as part of a medical evaluation.

Treatment of Sexual Offenders

The best approach to treatment of children and adolescents with mental retardation who have engaged in sexual offenses is a combination of interventions that are used with sex offenders in the general population, and strategies that address the particular requirements and limitations of the individual to be treated (Schilling & Schinke, 1989). It is especially important to make certain that the person understands the content of the material that focuses on sexual behaviors. The treatment approach must be primarily behavioral, concrete, practically oriented, action-oriented, and repetitive. In most instances, a group approach would be the treatment of choice, just as it is with other sex offenders, so that public acknowledgment of the behavior and peer pressure can be used to facilitate progress.

Some general guidelines for treatment (based on the work of Gilby et al., 1989; Schilling & Schinke, 1989; and Swanson & Garwick, 1990) include:

1	The social service delivery system often must be targeted to promote opportunities for normal sexual expression. The information gathered through consideration of Hingsburger et al.'s (1989) eleven hypotheses lead directly to intervention in the person's living, school, or work setting.
2	Coordination of any intervention program with other agencies involved with the sex offender is vital.
3	Community supports must be developed and tailored to meet the unique needs of the individual involved.
4	The range of behavioral problems and deficits exhibited by the person with mental retardation must be addressed in addition to the sexual problems.
5	Sexually offensive behavior must be replaced with alternative, appropriate sexual behavior.
6	The person must learn to discriminate between appropriate and inappropriate sexual behavior, learn about appropriate social–sexual relationships, and take personal responsibility for the sexual offense. When possible, it also is desirable to develop empathy for the victim(s), gain self-control, learn how to self-monitor through learning about the precipitating factors and motivations for the abusive behavior, and learn to avoid tempting situations.
7	Deviant arousal patterns and fantasies (which are less frequent in the person with mental retardation) may have to be eliminated with a combination of aversive and positive behavioral techniques.

In summary, the little data that is available indicates that adolescents with mild to moderate mental retardation engage in sexual offenses at about the same rate as adolescents in the general poppulation. The basis for this behavior in the adolescent with mental retardation, however, can be the result of societal attitudes, living circumstances, and developmental deficits which limit opportunities for learning or engaging in normative social and sexual relationships. These factors must be taken into account in order to differentiate sexually deviant behaviors from sexual behaviors that are inappropriate but not deviant. Regardless of the factors that may contribute to the behavior, the seriousness of sexually offensive behavior cannot be ignored in adolescents with mental retardation. Sexual offenses are not uncommon for adolescents with or without mental retardation, and must be treated to prevent their escalation into more violent sexual offenses and, most importantly, to protect the victims from pain and suffering. The importance of understanding and treating the sexual offenses within the context of the person's unique developmental and social needs, the circumstances of the abuse, and the relationship of the sexually abusive behavior to other aggressive behavior cannot be overemphasized. For some adolescent offenders with mental retardation, treatment goals may be necessarily limited by the nature and severity of the disability and the sexual behaviors. In these cases, a controlled living environment may be the only way to protect others from being victimized.

References

Abidin, R. R. (1990). *Parenting stress index manual* (3rd ed.). Charlottesville, VA: Pediatric Psychology Press.

Achenbach, T. M., & Edelbrock, C. S. (1981). Behavioral problems and competencies reported by parents of normal and disturbed children aged 4 through 16. *Monographs of the Society for Research in Child Development, 46,* (Serial No. 188).

Achenbach, T. M., & Edelbrock, C. S (1983). *Manual for the child behavior checklist and revised child behavior profile.* Burlington, VT: University Associates in Psychiatry.

Adams, C., & Fay, J. (1992). *Helping your child recover from sexual abuse.* Seattle, WA: University of Washington Press.

Alter-Reid, K., Gibbs, M., Lachenmeyer, J., Sigal, J., & Massoth, N. (1986). Sexual abuse of children: A review of the empirical findings. *Journal of Clinical Psychology Review, 6,* 249–266.

American Academy of Child and Adolescent Psychiatry (1988). Guidelines for the clinical evaluation of child and adolescent sexual abuse. *Journal of the American Academy of Child and Adolescent Psychiatry, 27,* 655–657.

American Professional Society on the Abuse of Children (1990). *Guidelines for psychosexual evaluation of childhood sexual abuse in young children.* Chicago, IL: Author.

American Psychiatric Association. (1987). *Diagnostic and statistical manual of mental disorders* (3rd ed. rev.). Washington, DC: Author.

American Psychiatric Association (1994). *Diagnostic and statistical manual of mental disorders* (4th ed.). Washington, DC: Author.

American Psychological Association (1994). *Report of the anatomical doll task force.* Washington, DC: Author.

Anderson, D., & Finn, M. (1986). *Margaret's story: Sexual abuse and going to court.* Minneapolis, MN: Dillon Press.

Awad, G. A., & Saunders, E. B. (1989). Adolescent child molesters: Clinical observations. *Child Psychiatry and Human Development, 19,* 195–206.

Bagley, C. (1990). Is the prevalence of child sexual abuse decreasing? Evidence from a random sample of 750 young adult women. *Psychological Reports, 66,* 1037–1038.

Baker-Ward, L. E., Gordon, B. N., Ornstein, P. A., Larus, D., & Clubb, P. A. (1993). Young children's long-term retention of a pediatric examination. *Child Development, 64,* 1519–1533.

Baker-Ward, L. E., Hess, T. M., & Flanagan, D. A. (1990). The effects of involvement on children's memory for events. *Cognitive Development, 5,* 55–70.

Beaudry, J., & Ketchum, L. (1987). *Carla goes to court.* New York: Human Sciences Press.

Becker, J. V. (1988). The effects of child sexual abuse on adolescent sexual offenders. In G. E. Wyatt, & G J. Powell (Eds.), *Lasting effects of child sexual abuse* (pp. 193–207). Beverly Hills: Sage.

Beitchman, J. H., Zucker, K. J., Hood, J. E., DaCosta, G. A., Akman, D., & Cassavia, E. (1991). A review of the short-term effects of child sexual abuse. *Child Abuse & Neglect, 15*, 537–556.

Beitchman, J. H., Zucker, K. J., Hood, J. E., DaCosta, G. A., Akman, D., & Cassavia, E. (1992). A review of the long-term effects of child sexual abuse. *Child Abuse & Neglect, 16*, 101–118.

Bell, A. P., Weinberg, M. A., & Hammersmith, S. K. (1981). *Sexual preference: Its development in men and women.* Bloomington, IL: Indiana University Press.

Bellamy, G. T., Clark, G. M., Hamre-Nietupski, S., & Williams, W. (1977). Habilitation. *Education and Training of the Mentally Retarded, 12*, 364–372.

Bem, S. L. (1989). Genital knowledge and gender constancy in preschool children. *Child Development, 60*, 649–662.

Berliner, L., & Conte, J. R. (1993). Sexual abuse evaluations: Conceptual and empirical obstacles. *Child Abuse & Neglect, 17*, 111–125.

Berliner, L., & Ernst, E. (1984). Group work with preadolescent sexual assault victims. In I. R. Stuart & J. G. Greer (Eds.), *Victims of sexual aggression: Treatment of children, women, and men* (pp. 105–124). New York: Van Nostrand Reinhold.

Bernstein, A. C., & Cowen, P. A. (1975). Children's concepts of how people get babies. *Child Development, 46*, 77–91.

Blanchard, R. (1990). Gender identity disorders in adult men. In R. Blanchard & B. W. Steiner (Eds.), *Clinical management of gender identity disorders in children and adults* (pp. 47–76). Washington, DC: American Psychiatric Press.

Blanchard, R., Clemmensen, L. H., & Teiner, B. W. (1987). Heterosexual and homosexual gender dysphoria. *Archives of Sexual Behavior, 16*, 139–152.

Blick, L. C., & Porter, F. S. (1982). Group therapy with female adolescent incest victims. In S. M. Sgroi (Ed.), *Handbook of clinical intervention in child sexual abuse* (pp. 147–175). Lexington, MA: Lexington Books.

Boat, B. W., & Everson, M. D. (1994). Exploration of anatomical dolls by nonreferred preschool-aged children: Comparisons by age, gender, race, and socioeconomic status. *Child Abuse & Neglect, 18*, 139–153.

Brainerd, C. J., & Ornstein, P. A. (1991). Children's memory for witnessed events: The developmental backdrop. In J. Doris (Ed.), *The suggestibility of children's recollections: Implications for eyewitness testimony* (pp. 10–20). Washington, DC: American Psychological Association.

Brantlinger, E. A. (1985). Mildly mentally retarded secondary students' information about and attitudes toward sexuality and sexuality education. *Education and Training of the Mentally Retarded, 20*, 99–108.

Brantlinger, E. A. (1988). Teachers' perceptions of the sexuality of their secondary students with mild mental retardation. *Education and Training in Mental Retardation, 23*, 24–37.

Brooks-Gunn, J., & Warren, M. P. (1988). The psychological significance of secondary sexual characteristics in nine- to eleven-year-olds girls. *Child Development, 59*, 1061–1069.

Brown, E., Flanagan, T., & McLeod, M. (Eds.). (1984). *Sourcebook of criminal justice statistics—1983.* Washington, DC: Bureau of Justice Statistics.

Browne, A., & Finkelhor, D. (1986). Impact of child sexual abuse: A review of the research. *Psychological Bulletin, 99*, 66–77.

Budin, L. E., & Johnson, C. F. (1989). Sex abuse prevention programs: Offenders' attitudes about their efficacy. *Child Aubse & Neglect, 13*, 77–87.

Calderone, M. S., & Johnson, E. W. (1983). *The family book about sexuality* (rev. ed.). New York: Bantam Books.

Ceci, S. J., & Bruck, M. (1993). Suggestibility of the child witness: A historical review and synthesis. *Psychological Bulletin, 113*, 403–439.

Ceci, S. J., Leichtman, M. D., & White, T. (in press). Interviewing perschoolers: Rememberance of things planted. In D. Peters (Ed.), *The child witness in context: Cognitive, social, and legal perspectives*. Amsterdam, Netherlands: Kluwer.

Ceci, S. J., Ross, D. F., & Toglia, M. P. (1987a). Suggestibility of children's memory: Psycholegal implications. *Journal of Experimental Psychology: General, 116*, 38–49.

Ceci, S. J., Ross, D. F., & Toglia, M. P. (1987b). Age differences in suggestibility: Narrowing the uncertainties. In S. J. Ceci, M. P. Toglia, & D. F. Ross (Eds.), *Children's eyewitness testimony* (pp. 79–91). New York: Springer-Verlag.

Chamberlain, A., Rauh, J., Passer, A., McGrath, M., & Burket, R. (1984). Issues in fertility control for mentally retarded female adolescents: I. Sexual activity, sexual abuse and contraception. *Pediatrics, 73*, 445–450.

Chi, M. T., Glasser, R., & Farr, M. (Eds.). (1988). *The nature of experience*. Hillsdate, NJ: Erlbaum.

Clarke-Stewart, A., Thompson, W. C., & Lepore, S. (1989, April). Manipulating children's interpretations through interrogation. In G. S. Goodman (Chair), *Can children provide accurate eyewitness reports:* Symposium conducted at the biennial meeting of the Society for Research in Child Development, Kansas City, MO.

Clubb, P. A., & Ornstein, P. A. (1992, April). Visiting the doctor: Children's differential retention of individual components of the physical examination. In D. Bjorklund & P. A. Ornstein (Chairs). *Children's memory for real-world events: Implications for testimony*. Symposium presented at the Conference on Human Development, Atlanta, GA.

Coates, S., & Person, E. S. (1985). Extreme boyhood femininity: Isolated behavior or pervasive disorder? *Journal of the American Academy of Child and Adolescent Psychiatry, 24*, 702–709.

Committee for Children. (1989). *Second step: A violence prevention curriculum*. (Available from Committee for Children, 172 20th Avenue, Seattle, WA 98122.)

Conte, J. R., Wolf, S., & Smith, T. (1989). What sexual offenders tell us about prevention strategies. *Child Abuse & Neglect, 13*, 293–335.

Corder, B. F., Haizlip, T., & DeBoer, P. (1990). A pilot study for a structured, time-limited therapy group for sexually abused pre-adolescent children. *Child Abuse & Neglect, 14*, 243–251.

Craft, A., & Craft, M. (1978). *Sex and the mentally handicapped*. London: Routledge & Kegan Paul.

Craft, A., & Craft, M. (1979). *Handicapped married couples*. London: Routledge & Kegan Paul.

Craig, M. E. (1990). Coercive sexuality in dating relationships: A situational model. *Clinical Psychology Review, 10*, 395–423.

Crowder, R. G. (1976). *Principles of learning and memory*. Hillsdale, NJ: Erlbaum.

Cruz, V. K., Price-Williams, D., & Andron, L. (1988). Developmentally disabled women who were molested as children. *Social Casework, 69*, 411–419.

Damon, L., Todd, J., & Macfarlane, K. (1987). Treatment issues with sexually abused young children. *Child Welfare, 66*, 125–137.

Davis, G. E., & Leitenberg, J. (1987). Adolescent sex offenders. *Psychological Bulletin, 101*, 417–427.

Davis, M. (1989). Gender and sexual development of women with mental retardation. *The Disabilities Studies Quarterly, 9*, 19–20.

DeLoache, J. S., & Marzolf, D. P. (1993, March). *Young children's testimony may not be improved by using dolls to question them*. Poster presented at the biennial meeting of the Society for Research in Child Development, New Orleans, LA.

deYoung, M. (1987). Disclosing sexual abuse: The impact of developmental variables. *Child Welfare, 66*, 217–223.

Doll, L. S., Joy, D., Bartholow, B. N., Harrison, J. S., Bolan, G., Douglas, J. M., Saltzman,

L. E., Moss, P. M., & Delgado, W. (1992). Self-reported childhood and adolescent sexual abuse among adult homosexual and bisexual men. *Child Abuse & Neglect, 16,* 855–864.

Downing, J., Jenkins, S. J., & Fisher, G. L. (1988). A comparison of psychodynamic and reinforcement treatment with sexually abused children. *Elementary School Guidance and Counseling, 22,* 291–298.

Edgerton, R. B. (1973). Some socio-cultural research considerations. In F. F. de la Cruz & G. D. LaVeck (Eds.), *Human sexuality and the mentally retarded* (pp. 240–249). New York: Bruner/Mazel.

Edgerton, R. B., & Dingman, H. (1964). Good reasons for bad supervision: Dating in a hospital for mentally retarded. *Psychiatric Quarterly Supplement, Part 2,* 221–223.

Edmonson, B., McCombs, K., & Wish, J. (1979). What retarded adults believe about sex. *American Journal of Mental Deficiency, 84,* 11–18.

Elliott, D. S., & Morse, B. J. (1989). Delinquency and drug use as risk factors in teenage sexual activity. *Youth and Society, 21,* 32–57.

Elvik, S. L., Berkowitz, C. D., Nicholas, E., Lipman, J. L., & Inkelis, S. H. (1990). Sexual abuse in the developmentally disabled: Dilemmas of diagnosis. *Child Abuse & Neglect, 14,* 497–502.

Evans, A. L., & McKinlay, I. A. (1988). Sexual maturation in girls with severe mental handicap. *Child Care, Health and Development, 14,* 59–69.

Everson, M. D., & Boat, B. W. (1989). False allegations of sexual abuse by children and adolescents. *Journal of the American Academy of Child and Adolescent Psychiatry, 28,* 230–235.

Everson, M. D., & Boat, B. W. (1990). Sexualized doll play among young children: Implications for the use of anatomical dolls in sexual abuse evaluations. *Journal of the American Academy of Child and Adolescent Psychiatry, 29,* 736–742.

Everson, M. D., & Boat, B. W. (1994). Putting the anatomical doll controversy in perspective: An examination of the major uses and criticisms of the dolls in child sexual abuse evaluations. *Child Abuse & Neglect, 18,* 113–129.

Faller, K. C. (1988). Criteria for judging the credibility of children's statements about their sexual abuse. *Child Welfare, 67,* 389–401.

Fehrenbach, P. A., Smith, W., Monastersky, C., & Deisher, R. W. (1986). Adolescent sexual offenders: Offender and offense characteristics. *American Journal of Orthopsychiatry, 56,* 225–233.

Finkel, M. L., & Finkel, D. G. (1981). Sexual and contraceptive knowledge, attitudes and behavior of male adolescents. In F. Furstenberg, R. Lincoln, & J. Menken (Eds.), *Teenage sexuality, pregnancy, and childbearing* (pp. 327–335). Philadelphia: Temple University Press.

Finkelhor, D. (1981). Sex between siblings: Sex play, incest, and aggression. In L. L. Constantine & F. M. Martinson (Eds.), *Children and sex: New findings, new perspectives* (pp. 129–149). Boston: Little, Brown.

Finkelhor, D. (1984). *Child sexual abuse: New theory and research.* New York: The Free Press.

Finkelhor, D. (1987). The sexual abuse of children: Current research reviewed. *Psychiatric Annals, 17,* 233–241.

Finkelhor, D., & Browne, A. (1985). Traumatic impact of child sexual abuse: A conceptualization. *American Journal of Orthopsychiatry, 55,* 530–541.

Finkelhor, D., Hotaling, G., Lewis, I. A., & Smith, C. (1990). Sexual abuse in a national survey of adult men and women: Prevalence, characteristics, and risk factors. *Child Abuse & Neglect, 14,* 19–28.

Finkelhor, D., Williams, L. M., & Burns, N. (1988). *Nursery crimes: Sexual abuse in day care.* Newbury Park, CA: Sage Publications.

Fischer, H. L., Krajicek, M. J., Borthick, W. A. (1973). *Sex education for the developmentally disabled: A guide for parents, teachers, and professionals.* Baltimore, MD: University Park Press.

Flavell, J. H. (1985). *Cognitive development* (2nd ed.). Englewood Cliffs, NJ: Prentice-Hall.

Follmer, A., & Gordon, B.N. (1994, April). Does enactment facilitate young children's reports of their medical examinations? In B.N. Gordon, (Chair), *Young children's accounts of medical and dental examinations: Remembering and reporting personal experiences.* Symposium presented at the biennial meeting of the Conference on Human Development, Pittsburgh, PA.

Friedrich, W. N. (1990). *Psychotherapy of sexually abused children and their families.* New York: W. W. Norton.

Friedrich, W. N., Beilke, R. L., & Urquiza, A. J. (1988). Brief diagnostic group treatment of sexually abused boys: A comparison study. *Journal of Interpersonal Violence, 3,* 21–28.

Friedrich, W. N., Grambsch, P., Broughton, D., Kuiper, J., & Beilke, R. L. (1991). Normative sexual behavior in children. *Pediatrics, 88,* 456–464.

Friedrich, W., Grambsch, P., Damon, L., Koverola, C., Wolfe, V. Hewitt, S., Lang, R., & Broughton, D. (1992). The Child Sexual Behavior Inventory: Normative and clinical comparisons. *Psychological Assessment, 4,* 303–311.

Friedrich, W. N. Jaworski, T. M., Huxsahl, J. E., & Bengtson, B. S. (1994). *Dissociative and sexual behaviors in children and adolescents with sexual abuse and psychiatric histories.* Manuscript under review.

Friedrich, W. N., Luecke, W. J., Beilke, R. L., & Place, V. (1992). Psychotherapy outcome of sexually abused boys. *Journal of Interpersonal Violence, 7,* 396–409.

Gale, J., Thompson, R. J., Moran, T. & Sack, W. H. (1988). Sexual abuse in young children: Its clinical presentation and characteristic patterns. *Child Abuse & Neglect, 12,* 163–170.

Garbarino, J. (1988). Preventing childhood injury: Developmental and mental health issues. *American Journal of Orthopsychiatry, 58,* 25–45.

Gebhard, P. H. (1973). Sexual behavior of the mentally retarded. In F. F. de la Cruz & G. D. LaVeck (Eds.), *Human sexuality and the mentally retarded* (pp. 29–50). New York: Bruner/Mazel.

Geiselman, R. E., Saywitz, K. J., & Bornstein, G. K. (1993). Effects of cognitive questioning techniques on children's recall performance. In G. S. Goodman & B. L. Bottoms (Eds.), *Child victims, child witnesses; Understanding and improving testimony* (pp. 71–94). New York: Guilford Press.

Gewirtz, J. L., Weber, R. A., & Nogueras, M. (1990, April). *The role of facial characteristics in neonatal gender discrimination with photographs.* Paper presented at the International Conference on Infant Studies, Montreal, Canada.

Gil, E. (1993). Age-appropriate sex play versus problematic sexual behaviors. In E. Gil & T. C. Johnson (Eds.). *Sexualized children: Assessment and treatment of sexualized children and children who molest* (pp. 21–39). Rockville, MD: Launch Press.

Gil, E., & Johnson, T. C. (1993). *Sexualized children: Assessment and treatment of sexualized children and children who molest.* Rockville, MD: Launch Press.

Gilby, R., Wolf, L., & Goldberg, B. (1989). Mentally retarded adolescent sex offenders: A survey and pilot study. *Canadian Journal of Psychiatry, 34,* 542–548.

Gordon, B. N., & Follmer, A. (1994). Developmental issues in judging the credibility of children's testimony. *Journal of Clinical Child Psychology, 23,* 283–294.

Gordon, B. N., Ornstein, P. A., Nida, R. E., Follmer, A., Crenshaw, M. C., & Albert, G. (1993). Does the use of dolls facilitate children's memory of visits to the doctor: *Applied Cognitive Psychology, 7,* 459–474.

Gordon, B. N., Schroeder, C. S., & Abrams, J. M. (1990a). Age and social-class differences in children's knowledge of sexuality. *Journal of Clinical Child Psychology, 19,* 33–43.

Gordon, B. N., Schroeder, C. S., & Abrams, J. M. (1990b). Children's knowledge of sexuality: A comparison of sexually abused and nonabused children. *American Journal of Orthopsychiatry, 60,* 250–257.

Gordon, B. N., Schroeder, C. S., Ornstein, P. A., & Baker-Ward, L. E. (in press). Clinical implications of research on memory development. In T. Ney (Ed.), *Allegations in child sexual abuse: Assessment and case management.* New York: Brunner/Mazel.

Gordon, S. (1978). *Facts about sex for today's youth.* Fayetteville, NY: Ed-U Press.

Gordon, S. (1983). *Girls are girls and boys are boys so what's the difference? A nonsexist sexuality education book for children age 6 to 10.* Fayetteville, NY: Ed-U Press.

Gordon, S., & Gordon, J. (1974). *Did the sun shine before you were born: A sex education primer.* New York: Joseph Okpaku.

Gordon, S., & Gordon, J. (1984). *A better safe than sorry book: A family guide for sexual assault prevention.* Fayetteville, NY: Ed-U Press.

Gordon, S., & Snyder, S. V. (1983). Sex education. In C. E. Walker & M. C. Roberts (Eds.), *Handbook of clinical child psychology* (pp. 1154–1173). New York: Wiley.

Green, R. (1985). Gender identity in childhood and later sexual orientation: Follow-up of 78 males. *American Journal of Psychiatry, 142,* 339–341.

Green, R. (1987). *The ''sissy boy syndrome'' and the development of homosexuality.* New Haven: Yale University Press.

Gudjonsson, G. H., & Gunn, J. (1982). The competence and reliability of a witness in a criminal court: A case report. *British Journal of Psychiatry, 141,* 624–627.

Gundersen, B. H., Melas, P. S., & Skar, J. E. (1981). Sexual behavior of preschool children. In L. L. Constantine & F. M. Martinson (Eds.), *Children and sex: New findings, new perspectives* (pp. 45–72). Boston: Little, Brown.

Hall, G. C. N. (1990). Prediction of sexual aggression. *Clinical Psychology Review, 10,* 229–245.

Hall, J. (1975). Sexuality and the mentally retarded. In R. Green (Ed.), *Human sexuality: A health practitioner's text* (pp. 181–195). Baltimore: Williams & Wilkins.

Hanson, R. K., Steffy, R. A., & Gauthier, R. (1993). Long-term recidivism of child molesters. *Journal of Consulting and Clinical Psychology, 61,* 646–652.

Haroian, L. M. (1991). Sexual problems of children. In M. Roberts & E. Walker (Eds.), *Handbook of clinical child psychology 2nd ed.* (pp. 431–450). New York: Wiley.

Harter, S. (1983). *Supplementary description of the Self-Perception Profile for Children: Revision of the Perceived Competence Scale for Children.* Unpublished manuscript, University of Denver.

Harter, S., & Pike, R. (1984). The Pictorial Scale of Perceived Competence and Social Acceptance for Young Children. *Child Development, 55,* 1969–1982.

Hayes, C. D. (1987). *Risking the future: Adolescent sexuality, pregnancy, and childbearing* (Vol. 1). Washington, DC: National Academy Press.

Healy, N., Fitzpatrick, C., & Fitzgerald, E. (1991). Clinical note: Childhood neurotic disorders with a sexual content need not imply child sexual abuse. *Journal of Child Psychology and Psychiatry, 32,* 857–863.

Hewitt, S. K. (1991). Therapeutic management of preschool cases of alleged but unsubstantiated sexual abuse. *Child Welfare, 70,* 59–67.

Hingsburger, D., Griffiths, D., & Quinsey, V. (1991). Detecting counterfeit deviance: Differentiating sexual deviance from sexual inappropriateness. *The Habilitative Mental Healthcare Newsletter, 10,* 51–54.

Hoier, T., Inderbitzer-Pisaruk, H., & Shawchuck, C. (1988). *Short-term cognitive behavioral group treatment for victims of sexual abuse.* Unpublished manuscript, West Virginia University, Department of Psychology, Morgantown.

Howe, S. G. (1976). On the causes of idiocy. In M. Rosen, G. R. Clark, & M. S. Kivitz (Eds.), *The history of mental retardation: Collected papers* (Vol. 1, pp. 31–60). Baltimore: University Park Press.

Huntley, C. F., & Benner, S. M. (1993). Reducing barriers to sex education for adults with mental retardation. *Mental Retardation, 31,* 215–220.

Inderbitzen-Pisaruk, H., Shawchuck, C. R., & Hoier, T. S. (1992). Behavioral characteristics of child victims of sexual abuse: A comparison study. *Journal of Clinical Child Psychology, 21,* 14–19.

Jay, S. M. (1988). Invasive medical procedures: Psychological intervention and assessment. In D. K. Routh (Ed.), *Handbook of pediatric psychology* (pp. 401–425). New York: Guilford Press.

Johnson, T. C. (1988). Child perpetrators: Children who molest other children, preliminary findings. *Child Abuse & Neglect, 12,* 219–229.

Johnson, T. C. (1989). Female child perpetrators: Children who molest other children. *Child Abuse & Neglect, 13,* 571–585.

Karacan, I., Rosenbloom, A. L., & Williams, R. L. (1970). The clitoral erection cycle during sleep. *Psychophysiology, 7,* 338.

Katz, R. C. (1990). Psychosocial adjustment in adolescent child molesters. *Child Abuse & Neglect, 14,* 567–575.

Kauli, R., Prager-Lewin, R., & Laron, A. (1978). Pubertal development in the Prader-Labhart-Willi syndrome. *Acta Paediatrica Scandinavica, 67,* 763–767.

Kempton, T., & Forehand, R. (1992). Juvenile sex offenders: Similar to, different from other incarcerated delinquent offenders? *Behavior Research and Therapy, 30,* 533–536.

Kendall-Tackett, K. A., Williams, L. M., & Finkelhor, D. (1993). Impact of sexual abuse on children: A review and synthesis of recent empirical studies. *Psychological Bulletim, 113,* 164–180.

Kinsey, A. C., Pomeroy, W. B., & Martin, C. E. (1948). *Sexual behavior in the human male.* Philadelphia: Saunders.

Klein, M., & Gordon, S. (1991). Sex education. In C. E. Walker & M. M. Roberts (Eds.), *Handbook of clinical child psychology, rev. ed.* (pp. 933–949). New York: Wiley.

Koblinsky, S. A. (1983). *Sexuality education for parents of young children.* New York: Ed-U Press.

Kolko, D. J. (1988). Educational programs to promote awareness and prevention of child sexual victimization: A review and methodological critique. *Clinical Psychology Review, 8,* 195–209.

Lamb, M. E. (1994). The investigation of child sexual abuse: An interdisciplinary consensus statement. *Expert Evidence, 2,* 151–156.

Lamb, S., & Coakley, M. (1993). "Normal" childhood sexual play and games: Differentiating play from abuse. *Child Abuse & Neglect, 17,* 515–526.

Laws, D. R. (Ed.). (1989). *Relapse prevention with sex offenders.* New York: Guilford Press.

Levy, S. R., Perhats, C., Nash-Johnson, M., & Welter, J. F. (1992). Reducing the risks in pregnant teens who are very young and those with mild mental retardation. *Mental Retardation, 30,* 195–203.

Lie, G., & McMurtry, S. L. (1991). Foster care for sexually abused children: A comparative study. *Child Abuse & Neglect, 15,* 111–121.

Lindsay, D. S., & Read, J. D. (1994). Psychotherapy and memories of childhood sexual abuse: A cognitive perspective. *Applied cognitive psychology, 8,* 281–338.

Loftus, E. F. (1979). *Eyewitness testimony.* Cambridge: Harvard University Press.

Loftus, E. F. (1993). The reality of repressed memories. *American Psychologist, 48,* 518–537.

Lombardo, P. (1982). *Eugenic sterlization in Virginia: Aubrey Strode and the case of Buck v. Bell.* Unpublished dissertation, University of Virginia, Charlottesville, VA.

Mandler, J. M. (1990). Recall and its verbal expression. In R. Fivush & J. A. Hudson (Eds.), *Knowing and remembering in young children* (pp. 317–330). New York: Cambridge University Press.

Mansell, S., Sobsey, D., & Calder, P. (1992). Sexual abuse treatment for persons with developmental disabilities. *Professional Psychology: Research and Practice, 23,* 404–409.

Marantz, S., & Coates, S. (1991). Mothers of boys with gender identity disorder: A comparison of matched controls. *Journal of the American Academy of Child and Adolescent Psychiatry, 30,* 310–315.

Margolin, L. (1991). Child sexual abuse by nonrelated caregivers. *Child Abuse & Neglect, 15,* 213–221.

Marshall, W. L., Laws, D. R., & Barbaree, H. E. (Eds.). (1990). *Handbook of sexual assault: Issues, theories and treatment of the offender.* New York: Plenum.

Martinson, F. M. (1981). Eroticism in infancy and childhood. In L. L. Constantine & F. M. Martinson (Eds.), *Children and sex: New findings, new perspectives* (pp. 23–35). Boston: Little, Brown.

Matson, J. L. (1984). Psychotherapy with persons who are mentally retarded. *Mental Retardation, 22,* 170–175.

McArthur, D. S. & Roberts, G. E. (1982). *Roberts' apperception test for children.* Los Angeles: Western Psychological Services.

McCabe, M. P. (1993). Sex education programs for people with mental retardation: Are they necessary? *Mental Retardation, 31,* 377–387.

McCabe, M. P., & Schreck, A. (1992). Before sex education: An evaluation of the sexual knowledge experience, feeling and needs of people with mild intellectual disabilities. *Australia and New Zealand Journal of Developmental Disabilities, 18,* 75–82.

McConaghy, M. J. (1979). Gender permanence and the genital basis of gender: Stages in the development of constancy of gender identity. *Child Development, 50,* 1223–1226.

McLeer, S. V., Deblinger, E., Atkins, M. S., Foa, E. B., & Ralphe, D. L. (1988). Post-traumatic stress disorder in sexually abused children. *Journal of the American Academy of Child and Adolescent Psychiatry, 27,* 650–654.

McLeer, S. V., Deblinger, E., Henry, D., & Orvaschel, H. (1992). Sexually abused children at high risk for post-traumatic stress disorder. *Journal of the American Academy of Child and Adolescent Psychiatry, 31,* 875–879.

Melton, G. B., & Scott, E. S. (1984). Evaluation of mentally retarded persons for sterilization: Contributions and limits of psychological consultation. *Professional Psychology: Research and Practice, 15,* 34–48.

Merritt, K. A., Spiker, B., & Ornstein, P. A. (1993, March). *Distress and memory: Implications for autobiographical recall.* Paper presented at the biennial meeting of the Society for Research in Child Development, New Orleans, LA.

Meyer-Bahlburg, H. F. L. (1985). Gender identity disorder of childhood: Introduction. *Journal of the American Academy of Child Psychiatry, 24,* 681–683.

Meyer-Bahlburg, H. F. L., Ehrhardt, A. A., Bell, J. J., Cohen, S. F., Healey, J. M., Feldman, J. F., Morishima, A., Baker, S. W., & New, M. I. (1985). Idiopathic precocious puberty in girls. *Journal of Youth and Adolescence, 14,* 339–353.

Money, J. (1994). *Sex errors of the body and related syndromes: A guide to counseling children, adolescents, and their families* (2nd ed.). Baltimore, MD: Paul Brookes.

Money, J., Devore, H., & Norman, B. F. (1986). Gender identity and gender transposition: Longitudinal study of 32 male hermaphrodites assigned as girls. *Journal of Sex and Marital Therapy, 12,* 165–181.

Money, J., & Ehrhardt, A. A. (1972). *Man and woman, boy and girl: The differentiation and dimorphism of gender identity from conception to maturity.* Baltimore, MD: Johns Hopkins Press.

Money, J., & Norman, B. F. (1987). Gender identity and gender transposition: Longitudinal outcome study of 24 male hermaphrodites assigned as boys. *Journal of Sex and Marital Therapy, 13,* 75–92.

Money, J., & Russo, A. J. (1979). Homosexual outcome of discordant gender identity/role in childhood. *Journal of Pediatric Psychology, 4,* 29–41.

Morrison, D. (1989). Predicting contraceptive efficacy: A discriminant analysis of three groups of adolescent women. *Journal of Applied Social Psychology, 19,* 1431–1452.

Muehlenhard, C., & Linton, M. (1987). Date rape and sexual aggression in dating situations: Incidence and risk factors. *Journal of Counseling Psychology, 34,* 186–196.

Murphy, J. L. & Hinnes, P. M. (1994). Staff attitudes toward the sexuality of persons with intellectual disability. *Australia and New Zealand Journal of Developmental Disabilities, 19,* 45–52.

Murphy, W. D., Coleman, E. M., & Abel, G. G. (1983). Human sexuality in the mentally retarded. In J. L. Matson & F. Andrasik (Eds.), *Treatment issues and innovations in mental retardation* (pp. 581–643). New York: Plenum.

Murrin, M. R., & Laws, D. R. (1990). The influence of pornography on sexual crimes. In W. L. Marshall, D. R. Laws, & H. E. Barbaree (Eds.), *Handbook of sexual assault: Issues, theories, and treatment of the offender* (pp. 73–91). New York: Plenum.

Myles-Worsley, M., Cromer, C. C., & Dodd, D. H. (1986). Children's preschool script reconstruction: Reliance on general knowledge as memory fades. *Developmental Psychology, 22,* 22–30.

Nelson, J. A. (1981). The impact of incest: Factors in self-evaluation. In L. L. Constantine & F. M. Martinson (Eds.), *Children and sex: New findings, new perspectives* (pp. 163–174). Boston: Little, Brown.

Nelson, K. (1986). *Event knowledge: Structure and function in development.* Hillsdale, NJ: Erlbaum.

O'Brien, M., & Bera, W. (1986). Adolescent sexual offenders: A descriptive typology. *Preventing Sexual Abuse, 1,* 1–4.

O'Donohue, W. T., & Elliott, A. N. (1992). Treatment of the sexually abused child: A review. *Journal of Clinical Child Psychology, 21,* 218–228.

Ornstein, P. A. (1991). Commentary: Putting interviewing in context. In J. Doris (Ed.), *Suggestibility of children's recollections: Implications for eyewitness testimony* (pp. 147–152). Washington, DC: American Psychological Association.

Ornstein, P. A., Larus, D., & Clubb, P. A. (1991). Understanding children's testimony: Implications of research on the development of memory. In R. Vasta (Ed.), *Annals of child development* (Vol. 8, pp. 145–176). London: Jessica Kingsley.

Ousley, O. Y., & Mesibov, G. B. (1991). Sexual attitudes and knowledge of high-functioning adolescents and adults with autism. *Journal of Autism and Developmental Disorders, 21,* 471–481.

Palmer, P. (1977a). *Liking myself.* San Luis Obispo, CA: Impact Press.

Palmer, P. (1977b). *The mouse, the monster, and me.* San Luis Obispo, CA: Impact Press.

Parker, H., & Parker, S. (1986). Father–daughter sexual abuse: An emerging perspective. *American Journal of Orthopsychiatry, 56,* 531–549.

Patterson, C. J. (1992). Children of lesbian and gay parents. *Child Development, 63,* 1025–1042.

Patterson, G. R., Reid, J. B., Jones, R. R., & Conger, R. E. (1975). *A social learning approach to family intervention, Vol 1: Families with aggressive children.* Eugene, OR: Castalia.

Pellegrin, A., & Wagner, W. G. (1990). Child sexual abuse: Factors affecting victims' removal from home. *Child Abuse & Neglect, 14,* 53–60.

Peters, S. D., Wyatt, G. E., & Finkelhor, D. (1986). Prevalence. In D. Finkelhor & Associates (Eds.), *A sourcebook on child sexual abuse* (pp. 15–59). Beverly Hills, CA: Sage Publications.

Peterson, L. (1989). Coping by children undergoing stressful medical procedures: Some conceptual, methodological, and therapeutic issues. *Journal of Consulting and Clinical Psychology, 57,* 380–387.

Pettit, R., Fegan, M. & Howie, P. (1990, September). *Interviewer effects of children's testimony.* Paper presented at the International Congress on Child Abuse and Neglect, Hamburg, Germany.

Pope, A. W., McHale, S. M., & Craighead, W. E. (1988). *Self-esteem enhancement with children and adolescents.* Elmsford, NY: Pergamon Press.

Quattrin, T., Aronica, S., & Mazur, T. (1990). Management of male pseudohermaphroditism: A case report spanning twenty-one years. *Journal of Pediatric Psychology, 15,* 699–709.

Rafkin, L. (1990). *Different mothers: Sons and daughters of lesbians talk about their lives.* San Francisco: Cleis Press.

Rand, C., Graham, D. L. R., & Rawlings, E. I. (1982). Psychological health and factors the court seeks to control in lesbian mother custody trials. *Journal of Homosexuality, 8,* 27–39.

Reed, E. W., & Reed, S. (1965). *Mental retardation: A family study.* Philadelphia: Saunders.

Reis, J., & Herz, E. (1989). An examination of young adolescents' knowledge of and attitude toward sexuality according to perceived contraceptive responsiblity. *Journal of Applied Social Psychology, 19,* 231–250.

Rekers, G. A. (1991). Development of problems of puberty and sex roles in adolescence. In C. E. Walker & M. C. Roberts (Eds.), *Handbook of clinical child psychology* (2nd ed., pp. 607–622).

Rekers, G. A., Kilgus, M., & Rosen, A.C. (1990). Long-term effects of treatment for childhood gender disturbance. *Journal of Psychology and Human Sexuality, 3,* 121–153.

Rekers, G. A., & Lovaas, O. I. (1974). Behavioral treatment of deviant sex-role behaviors in a male child. *Journal of Applied Behavior Analysis, 7,* 173–190.

Repucci, N. D., & Haugaard, J. J. (1989). Prevention of child sexual abuse: Myth or reality? *American Psychologist, 44,* 1266–1275.

Rhodes, R. (1993). Mental retardation and sexual expression: An historical perspective. *Journal of Social Work and Human Sexuality, 8,* 1–27.

Rice, M. E., Quinsey, V. L., & Harris, G. T. (1991). Sexual recidivism among child molesters released from a maximum security psychiatric institution. *Journal of Consulting and Clinical Psychology, 59,* 381–386.

Robinson, S. (1984). Effects of a sex education program on intellectually handicapped adults. *Australia and New Zealand Journal of Development Disabilities, 10,* 21–26.

Rosenfeld, A., Bailey, R., Siegel, B., & Bailey, G. (1986). Determining incestuous contact between parent and child: Frequency of children touching parents' genitals in a nonclinical population. *Journal of the American Academy of Child Psychiatry, 25,* 481–484.

Routh, D. K., & Schroeder, C. S. (1981). Masturbation and other sexual behaviors. In S. Gabel (Ed.), *Behavior problems of childhood* (pp. 387–392). New York: Grune & Stratton.

Runyon, D. K., Everson, M. D., Edelsohn, G. A., Hunter, W. M., & Coulter, M. L. (1988). Impact of legal intervention on sexually abused children. *Journal of Pediatrics, 113,* 647–653.

Russ, R. J. (1990). *Keys to caring: Assisting our gay and lesbian clients.* Boston: Alyson Publications.

Russell, D. (1983). The incidence and prevalence of intrafamilial and extrafamilial sexual abuse of female children. *Child Abuse & Neglect, 7,* 133–146.

Rust, J. O., & Troupe, P. A. (1991). Relationships of treatment of child sexual abuse with school achievement and self-concept. *Journal of Early Adolescence, 11,* 420–429.

Rutter, M. (1970). Normal psychosexual development. *Journal of Child Psychology and Psychiatry, 11,* 259–283.

Rutter, M. (1975). *Helping troubled children.* New York: Plenum.

Rutter, M., & Rutter, M. (1993). *Developing minds: Challenge and continuity across the life span.* New York: Basic Books.

Sanders, G. & Mullis, R. (1988). Family influences on sexual attitudes and knowledge as reported by college students. *Adolescence, 23,* 837–845.

Sanford, D. (1986). *I can't talk about it.* Hong Kong: Golden Honey Books.

Saunders, B. E. (1993, October). *Treating symptoms of fear and anxiety in abused children.* Paper presented at the Midwest Conference on Child Sexual Abuse and Incest. Middleton, WI.

Saywitz, K. J., Geiselman, R. E., & Bornstein, G. K. (1992). Effects of cognitive interviewing and practice on children's recall performance. *Journal of Applied Psychology, 17,* 744–756.

Saywitz, K. J., Goodman, G. S., Nicholas, E., & Moan, S. (1991). Children's memories of physical examinations involving genital touch: Implications for reports of child sexual abuse. *Journal of Consulting and Clinical Psychology, 59,* 682–691.

Saywitz, K. J., Nathanson, R., & Snyder, L. (in press). Credibility of child witnesses: The role of communicative competence. *Topics in Language Disorders.*

Schaefer, C. E., & Millman, H. L. (1981). *How to help children with common problems.* New York: Van Nostrand Reinhold.

Schilling, R. F., & Schinke, S. P. (1989). Mentally retarded sex offenders: Fact, fiction, and treatment.

Schroeder, C. S., & Gordon, B. N. (1991). *Assessment and treatment of childhood problems: A clinician's guide.* New York: Guilford Press.

Schulenberg, J. (1985). *Gay parenting: A complete guide for gay men and lesbians with children.* Garden City, NY: Anchor Books.

Scott-Jones, D., & White, A. B. (1990). Correlates of sexual activity in early adolescence. *Journal of Early Adolescence, 10,* 221–238.

Sgroi, S. (1982). *Handbook of clinical intervention in child sexual abuse.* Lexington, MA: Lexington Books.

Sgroi, S. (1989). Evaluation and treatment of sexual offense behavior in persons with mental retardation. In S. Sgroi (Ed.), *Vulnerable populations (Vol. 2): Sexual abuse treatment for children, adult survivors, offenders, and persons with mental retardation* (pp. 245–283). Lexington, MA: Lexington Books.

Shea, V., & Gordon, B. N. (1992). *A social and sexual education picture book for adolescents and young adults with mental retardation.* Clinical Center for the Study of Development and Learning, University of North Carolina, Chapel Hill, NC.

Siegal, M., Waters, L. J., & Dinwiddy, L. S. (1988). Misleading children: Causal attributions for inconsistency under repeated questioning. *Journal of Experimental Child Psychology, 45,* 438–456.

Siegel, D. J. (in press). Memory, trauma and psychotherapy: A cognitive science view. *Journal of Psychotherapy Practice and Research.*

Sigelman, C. K., Budd, E. C., Winer, J. L., Schoenrock, C. J., & Martin, P. W. (1982). Evaluating alternative techniques of questioning mentally retarded persons. *American Journal of Mental Deficiency, 86,* 511–518.

Simonds, J. F. (1980). Sexual behavior in retarded children and adolescents. *Journal of Developmental and Behavioral Pediatrics, 1,* 173–179.

Slaby, R. G., & Frey, K. S. (1975). Development of gender constancy and selective attention to same-sex models. *Child Development, 46,* 849–856.

Sobsey, D. (1994). *Violence and abuse in the lives of people with disabilities.* Baltimore: Paul Brookes.

Sonis, W. A., Comite, F., Pescovitz, O. H., Hench, K., Rahn, C. W., Cutler, G. B., Loriaux, D. L., & Klein, R. P. (1986). Biobehavioral aspects of precocious puberty. *Journal of the American Academy of Child Psychiatry, 25,* 647–679.

Springs, F. E., & Friedrich, W. N. (1992). Health risk behaviors and medical sequelae of childhood sexual abuse. *Mayo Clinics Proceedings, 67,* 527–532.

Stermac, L. E. & Segal, Z. V. (1989). Adult sexual contact with children: An examination of cognitive factors. *Behavior Therapy, 20,* 573–584.

Stoller, R. J. (1975). *Sex and gender (Vol. 2): The transsexual experiment.* London: Hogarth Press.

Stowell, J., & Dietzel, M. (1982). *My very own book about me.* Spokane, WA: Lutheran Social Services of Washington.

Swanson, C. K., & Garwick, G. B. (1990). Treatment for low-functioning sex offenders: Group therapy and interagency coordination. *Mental Retardation, 28,* 155–161.

Sweet, P. E. (1981). *Something happened to me.* Racine, WI: Mother Courage Press.

Symonds, C. L., Mendoza, M. J., & Harrell, W. C. (1981). Forbidden sexual behavior among kin. In L. L. Constantine & F. M. Martinson (Eds.), *Children and sex: New findings, new perspectives* (pp. 151–162). Boston: Little, Brown.

Tanner, J.M. (1962). *Growth at adolescence* (2nd ed.). Oxford, U.K.: Blackwell.

Tharinger, D., Horton, C. B., & Millea, S. (1990). Sexual abuse and exploitation of children and adults with mental retardation and other handicaps. *Child Abuse & Neglect, 14,* 301–312.

Thoennes, N., & Tjaden, P. E. (1990). The extent, nature, and validity of sexual abuse allegations in custody/visitation disputes. *Child Abuse & Neglect, 14,* 151–163.

Timmers, R. L., DuCharme, P., & Jacob, G. (1981). Sexual knowledge, attitudes, and behaviors of developmentally disabled living in a normalized apartment setting. *Sexuality and Disability, 4,* 27–39.

Tomono, U., Maki, U., Ito, M., & Nakada, U. (1983). Precocious puberty due to past meningitic hydrocephalus. *Brain and Development, 5,* 414–417.

Toomey, J. F. (1993). Final report of the Bawnmore Personal Development Programme: Staff attitudes and sexuality programme development in an Irish service organization for people with mental handicap. *Research in Developmental Disabilities, 14,* 129–144.

Wachter, D. (1983). *No more secrets for me.* Boston: Little, Brown.

Walker, C. E., Bonner, B. L., & Kaufman, K. L. (1988). *The physically and sexually abused child: Evaluation and treatment.* Elmsford, NY: Pergamon Press.

Ward, I. L. (1984). The prenatal stress syndrome: Current Status. *Psychoneuroendocrinology, 9*, 3–11.

Waterman, J. (1986). Developmental considerations. In K. MacFarlane & J. Waterman (Eds.), *Sexual abuse of young children: Evaluation and treatment* (pp. 15–29). New York: Guilford.

Watkins, B., & Bentovim, A. (1992). The sexual abuse of male children and adolescents: A review of current research. *Journal of Child Psychology and Psychiatry, 33*, 197–248.

Wehrspann, W. H., Steinhauer, P. D., & Klajner-Diamond, H. K. (1987). Criteria and methodology for assessing credibility of sexual abuse allegations. *Canadian Journal of Psychiatry, 32*, 615–623.

Whitam, F. L., & Mathy, R. M. (1986). *Male homosexuality in four societies: Brazil, Guatemala, the Philippines, and the United States.* New York: Praeger.

White, S. D., & DeBlassie, R. R. (1992). Adolescent sexual behavior. *Adolescence, 27*, 183–191.

Winkler, R. C. (1977). What types of sex-role behavior should behavior modifiers promote? *Journal of Applied Behavior Analysis, 10*, 549–552.

Wish, J. R., McCombs, K. F., & Edmonson, B. (1980). *The Sociosexual Knowledge and Attitude Test.* Chicago, IL: Stoelting.

Wurtele, S. K., (1990). Teaching personal safety skills to four-year-old children: A behavioral approach. *Behavior Therapy, 22*, 69–83.

Wurtele, S. K., Currier, L. L., Gillispie, E. I., & Franklin, C. F. (1991). The efficacy of a parent-implemented program for teaching preschoolers personal safety skills. *Behavior Therapy, 22*, 69–83.

Wurtele, S. K., Kast, L. S., & Melzer, A. M. (in press). Sexual abuse prevention education for young chyildren: A comparison of teachers and parents as instructors. *Child Abuse & Neglect.*

Wurtele, S. K., Kast, L. S., Miller-Perrin, C. L., & Kondrick, P. A. (1989). A comparison of programs for teaching personal safety skills to preschoolers. *Journal of Consulting and Clinical Psychology, 57*, 505–511.

Wurtele, S. K., & Miller, C. L. (1987). Children's conceptions of sexual abuse. *Journal of Clinical Child Psychology, 16*, 184–191.

Wurtele, S. K., & Miller-Perrin, C. L. (1992). *Preventing child sexual abuse: Sharing the responsibility.* Lincoln, NE: University of Nebraska Press.

Yuille, J. C., Hunter, R., Joffe, R., & Saparniuk, J. (1993). Interviewing children in sexual abuse cases. In G. S. Goodman & B. L. Bottoms (Eds.), *Child victims, child witnesses: Understanding and improving testimony* (pp. 95–116). New York: Guilford Press.

Zucker, K. J. (1990a). Gender identity disorders in children. In R. Blanchard & B. W. Steiner (Eds.), *Clinical management of gender identity disorders in children and adults* (pp. 3–23). Washington, DC: American Psychiatric Press.

Zucker, K. J. (1990b). Psychosocial and erotic development in cross-gender identified children. *Canadian Journal of Psychiatry, 35*, 487–495.

Zucker, K. J. (1990c). Treatment of gender identity disorders in children. In R. Blanchard & B. W. Steiner (Eds.), *Clinical management of gender identity disorders in children and adults* (pp. 27–45). Washington, DC: American Psychiatric Press.

Zucker, K. J., & Green, R. (1992). Psychosexual disorders in children and adolescents. *Journal of Child Psychology and Psychiatry, 33*, 107–151.

Index